JOYRIDE

JOYRIDE

To a Reunion at Kardamyli

TONY SCOTLAND

SHELF LIVES
2018

Published in 2018 by
Shelf Lives
The Pottery, Baughurst RG26 5SD

ISBN 978-0-9955503-3-9

Second impression

Designed in Cycles by Libanus Press, Marlborough
Printed and Bound by TJ International, Padstow

To

Billa Harrod (1911–2005)
Joan Leigh Fermor (1912–2003)
Coote Heber-Percy (1912–2001)
Paddy Leigh Fermor (1915–2011)
Freda Berkeley (1923–2016)

Keep Ithaka always in your mind.
Arriving there is what you are destined for.
But do not hurry the journey at all.

C. P. Cavafy, *Ithaka*
(trans. Edmund Keeley and Philip Sherrard)

CONTENTS

Coote Heber-Percy and Freda Berkeley, 1995 (Photo: Tony Scotland).

Introduction

It was raining in London on the morning of Wednesday the 3rd October 1990 when a white Rover, sinking on its suspension, pulled away from a mansion block in Bayswater, and set off for some autumn sun in the Peloponnese 2000 miles away.

On board were three spirited old ladies, stout and a little lame but bound together by decades of friendship and a sense of fun. All three had been married to celebrated men, and each had made her own small mark as a muse: two had been immortalised in English literature, and the third inspired an opera.

That their husbands had all been bisexual was hardly a coincidence: the interests and feelings of those in their social circle ranged beyond the conventional, and often settled on the sort of men who were likely to be amusing, attentive, understanding – and safe. Now they were widows, each living on her own, but rarely alone, for they all took as great a delight in other people as other people continued to take in them.

Their destination was the town of Kardamyli on the western edge of the wild and rugged Mani Peninsula in the southern Peloponnese; and their plan was to spend a fortnight with their old friends, Patrick Leigh Fermor, the charismatic travel writer and hero of the Greek Resistance, and his wife, Joan, in their almost legendary house above a cove in the Gulf of Messini.

The driver was Lady Dorothy Heber-Percy ('Coote') placid, practical and missing nothing. She was tall, large and oval-faced, with birdlike features and thick, round spectacles. Her manner was self-contained, composed and quietly authoritative, like a grand and kindly abbess. Coote was the model for Cordelia Flyte in *Brideshead Revisited* – the wise bird of the Marchmain family, the only one who ends up happy. Very old-fashioned herself, she was entirely tolerant of those who were not.

The map-reader, Lady (Wilhelmine) Harrod – 'Billa' – was direct and unpredictable, occasionally sharp, but warm at heart, funny and clever. Her husband, the economist Sir Roy Harrod, had died twelve years previously, but, as a pillar of architectural conservation, she was still campaigning for the preservation of mediaeval churches, particularly in Norfolk. In Nancy Mitford's comic novels, *The Pursuit of Love*, and *Love in a Cold Climate*, she is commemorated as the narrator, Fanny, who, like Billa herself, married an Oxford don, settled in an elegant house opposite the Ashmolean and presided

Billa Harrod, at home in Norfolk.

over a salon where she entertained generations of dons and undergraduates with generous hospitality and a sympathetic ear.

The youngest of the trio, the bewitching and warm-hearted Lady Berkeley – Freda – was the pin-up and confidante of generations of single gentlemen, and the outsider whose gift for friendship had inspired her husband, the composer Sir Lennox Berkeley, to write the biblical opera *Ruth*.

Coote and Billa had been driving out to Kardamyli to stay with Paddy and Joan almost annually for years. They and Joan (then Eyres-Monsell) had been central figures of the Bright Young Things satirised by Evelyn Waugh in *Vile Bodies*. Now all three were in their late seventies, wiser but no less game.

Freda, a mere 67, had met the others through her marriage at the end of the war. She had been a lonely and unhappy schoolgirl when the Bright Young Things were dressing up and talking cockney, drinking and taking drugs, racing around nighttime London on bizarre treasure hunts and dancing the *Black Bottom*. As a qualified driver, Freda could have taken her turn at the wheel on this European jaunt, but, although she was a determined character, she was profoundly unconfident, and had refused to drive since the day she passed her test. Partly from a natural nervousness and partly to test her friends' love, she preferred instead to depend on others – for driving as for everything else.

All three were seasoned travellers, but none as inveterate, adventurous or impervious to discomfort as Coote; nor as organised, for she had been a Flight Officer in the WAAF during the war, and an archivist at Christie's afterwards. The Rover was hers and she was proud of it – a five-door saloon, exactly twelve months old, with a 1.6 litre Honda engine, a leather and walnut interior by

Vanden Plas, masked headlights for Europe, and a sun-roof. Coote herself had carried out all the vehicle checks for the long drive. The tyres were sound and the pressures adjusted for a heavy load, oil, battery and petrol had been topped up, spare wheel inflated, jack and wheel brace were where they should be in the tool kit, wipers new, and washer bottle full, with an extra litre just in case.

Abandoning her large, romantic garden in North Norfolk, Billa had taken the train up to London the day before, and spent the night with Freda in her rambling flat in an Edwardian mansion block off Westbourne Grove. It had not been entirely comfortable because the heating was off, the guestroom was piled high with displaced furniture and paintings, and the floorboards were up for plumbing and electrical work – Freda herself had tripped, and gashed her foot a few days before. But Billa's crossness evaporated with a breakfast of fresh croissants and brioches from Pierre Péchon's patisserie around the corner.

Coote arrived punctually at 9 a.m., having driven up from her cottage at Faringdon in Oxfordshire. Very late in both their lives she had unwisely married the eccentric and volatile master of Faringdon, Robert Heber-Percy, whom she had known and quietly loved since their wild days before the war, when he earned his nickname, 'the Mad Boy' (or 'Horrid Madboy', as Cecil Beaton called him). The marriage could not, and did not, work: within a year Coote was back in her cottage again, and a year after that she was a widow.

Freda was the most recently widowed of the trio. Her husband had died eighteen months ago, and, though he was twenty years her senior, and suffering, at the end, from Alzheimer's Disease, their long marriage had been happy and fulfilling and she was still grieving. She was hoping that the drive to Kardamyli, in the company of two such true, old friends, would be an Ithakan expedition giving her time not only to enjoy the journey itself but to examine her feelings, and possibly to heal some wounds. For Coote it was a chance to revisit a part of Italy where she served as a WAAF officer during the war. Billa had a specific objective too – she had a message for Paddy Leigh Fermor from her friend, the Prince of Wales.

If Paddy's great walk through Central and Eastern Europe before the war had been an escape from convention and parental expectations (producing two classic travel books, and the raw material for a third), the three ladies' adventure was an escape from their elderly routines. They needed time away to reflect, privately but in one another's company, on the way their lives had turned out – on their marriages, their families, their friendship itself. Perhaps to wonder too what the future held – Freda from her perspective as a Catholic, Billa as an Anglican, Coote passively somewhere in between (but not the devout Catholic of her alter ego in *Brideshead Revisited*). For all three, visiting Paddy and Joan in Kardamyli was a pilgrimage – and the journey there a joyride. There was no hiding the fact that its accomplishment would have something of an elegiac flavour, for they were all reaching the end of their lives: after six decades of friendship, this could be a final reunion. But all five shared the positive outlook of their generation, and they saw it not as a coda but a celebration.

Coote Lygon, Robert Heber-Percy, Penelope Betjeman and Gerald Berners, at Faringdon, c. 1938.

I

Departure

When Coote sounded the horn outside Hereford Mansions, Freda and Billa took the clattering old lift down from the third floor to the hall, and hobbled out of the front door, leaning on their walking sticks, taking care down the wet and slippery steps to the car. They were followed by Freda's assistant, Jane Norman (retired from the theatre), and the porter who carried the cases and stowed them in the boot.

Billa, though the shortest of the three widows, bagged the front seat, spreading maps on her lap to indicate her right to the extra legroom; Coote, the largest and tallest, squeezed into the driving seat, not without some difficulty; while Freda, whose swollen foot deserved more space, arranged herself in the back with a bulging nosebag of titbits. They were used to making do, these ladies who had lived through the war: their maxim was 'never complain, never explain'.

Once they were all packed in, Jane handed Freda a large red notebook, and reminded her to 'write it all up', as Patrick Leigh Fermor himself would have done – and not to lose it, as he had lost all but one of the diaries of his famous trudge from the Hook of Holland to Constantinople in the 1930s.*

Once they were under way – heading for the Bayswater Road, then Vauxhall, Elephant & Castle and the south coast – Billa threw out a challenge. What did they make of the news? Why, Freda

* Freda duly kept up her red travel diary, and later gave it to Tony Scotland, who dips in and out of it throughout this present book.

Hereford Mansions, London W2 (Photo: Edesio Fernandes).

wondered, more eager than anxious – had something awful happened? German re-unification, explained Coote quietly from the driving seat, repeating what the *Today* programme had reported as she drove up to London: from today the Democratic Republic was officially part of the Federal Republic, and Berlin, which had been a divided city since the end of the war, was once again the capital of a united Germany. To these three old friends who remembered the division of Germany after the war, it seemed hardly possible that the Wall was down, the Cold War a thing of the past, and citizens of the GDR were free to cross the border into the West.*

It would be a terrible burden for Bonn, observed Billa, who had lived with an economist for forty years, and it sometimes showed.† Communist businesses would have to be rebuilt, she said, ownership rights cleared up, infrastructure renovated – and of course the West German Government would have to repair all the abandoned churches. Billa was an indefatigable campaigner for the preservation of mediaeval churches. In 1974 she and John Betjeman had set

* When Ukraine withdrew from the USSR on Boxing Day the following year Soviet Communism finally came to an end, and the Soviet empire dissolved into fifteen separate nations.

† Sir Roy Harrod had been Nuffield Professor of International Economics at Oxford, a pioneer of the theory of dynamic growth in economics, and an advocate of international institutions to prevent a return of the kind of monetary breakdown that had occurred in the 1930s.

up a crusading committee to save the abandoned churches of Norfolk from dereliction. This had evolved into a powerful and effective charity called the Norfolk Churches Trust, of which she was President and the Prince of Wales Patron. A devout Anglican, and a passionate Conservative, Billa was also by nature, and by marriage, a great believer in conversation, and talk was what she wanted now. But Freda was not interested in politics, and Coote had the driving to think about.

As the Sidcup Road crossed the South Circular, Coote asked Billa to watch out for signs to the M20. Freda, who had been dozing, took this to mean they were making good progress, and, rummaging in her bag, produced some of her favourite *pastéis de nata*. Guzzling Portuguese custard tartlets, all three ladies soon forgot German reunification as they sped along the motorway towards Folkestone, and the coast road for Dover Harbour.

At the hovercraft terminal they joined a long queue. The time was ten to midday. Little did they know that at almost that same moment a significant act of European union – as momentous, in its way, as German re-unification – was taking place under the Channel, a few miles from the Dover shore. Engineers working on the new tunnel were successfully boring a pilot-hole through the rock still dividing the French and British ends of the tunnel. This was the birth of no more than the service tunnel, but soon it would be possible for British rail travellers to reach France under the sea.*

What with the news from Germany and the Tunnel, the omens seemed propitious for the old friends' reunion in Greece.

As they waited at Customs, Coote pulled a leaflet from the pocket of the car door and read up on the history of their hovercraft, the SR.N4 *Princess Margaret* Mk3. That it had made an appearance in the James Bond film, *Diamonds are Forever*, left her unmoved; what

* It was not till four years later that the Channel Tunnel was officially opened by the Queen and President Mitterand, first in Calais and then in Folkestone, on 6 May 1994.

SR.N4 *Princess Margaret.*

she wanted was technical data. How many cars could the *Princess* carry? (Up to sixty, in a four-lane bay between the two passenger saloons). And passengers? (Just over 400).Where did cars drive on? (Up the bow ramp, immediately forward of the cockpit). How long would the crossing take? (About thirty minutes, at a cruising speed of about 65 knots).* While Coote buried herself in her homework, and Billa read her book, Freda went to find the Duty-free.

* Both the *Princess Margaret* and her larger sister craft, *Princess Anne*, were decommissioned and retired to the Hovercraft Museum at Lee-on-the-Solent in 2000. *Princess Margaret* has since been broken up.

II

Normandy

Coote had planned the route with meticulous care. She had worked with maps as a photographic interpreter during the war, so she knew rather more than north from south. Her strategy now was to follow as straight a line as possible from Calais south-east to Brindisi (for the ferry across to Greece), and from Igoumenitsa down to Kardamyli, driving 200 miles a day, on country roads, with 11 overnight stops including ferry crossings. She had plotted each day's drive, and had marked in her Michelin some possible hotels – central, small, modest – but she had made no bookings, so the party would not be tied down. A seasoned traveller herself, she knew this would give them the freedom to absorb the ambience of new places, and Billa and Freda had complete faith in her leadership. As for sights, the route took account of their shared interest in old buildings, especially churches and monasteries, remote villages and unspoiled countryside – and Freda's special passion for markets and shopping.

Leaving Calais behind them, Coote headed first for Reims. Carefully avoiding the A26 motorway, the fast and busy *Autoroute des Anglais*, she wove her way deftly through a complicated web of smaller roads. Shortly after Saint-Omer she picked up the D324 for Arras. Soon they found themselves in the rolling country of farms, woods and poppies where the solemn cemeteries of the Somme commemorate the four million soldiers who died on the Western Front in the First World War.

All three widows fell silent, remembering that Billa's father had been one of the Great War's first casualties. A career soldier, Captain Francis Cresswell, adjutant of the Norfolk Regiment, was killed in action during the Retreat from Mons in August 1914, when he was thirty-one – and Billa, back home in the Norfolk village of Docking, just three. As they passed between Arras and Douai, Billa pointed to a road sign and said that after the Armistice her father's remains had been retrieved from the battlefield where he fell, and re-interred in the British Cemetery at Auberchicourt, a little to the north of where they now were.*

After driving for miles past the regimented graves of Picardy and the scars of the terrible battlefields, some of them with trenches restored, the travellers had no taste for lunch. But, ravenous by teatime, they stopped for a sandwich at a service station.

Having covered 267 miles since leaving London, they arrived in Reims before nightfall and settled themselves at the centre of the city in the Continental Hotel – nothing special, though it called itself Grand. Freda and Coote shared a small room, and Billa, who liked her privacy and always got her way, had an even smaller one on her own.

Rising first thing, they had an early breakfast and made for the Cathedral before the tour groups. Freda, who never missed a curiosity, wanted to see the famous Smiling Angel, who fell from his niche on the west front under bombardment by the Germans in September 1914, only twelve days after Billa's father's death up on the Western Front. Though the statue crashed to the ground, the grin remained stubbornly intact; after the war the face was restored to the rest of the head, the head restored to the body and the statue put back in its niche.

From Reims they made for Vitry-le-François in the Marne, where

* In 1918 Billa's widowed mother, Barbara née ffolkes, married the Colonel of the Norfolks, General (later Sir) Peter Strickland, who had led the 1st Infantry Division at the Battle of the Somme and was later to become General Officer Commanding British Troops in Egypt.

Le sourire de Reims

they stopped for coffee in the main square in the sunshine, before buying saucisson, cheese and fruit for a picnic – their lunchtime ritual for the rest of the journey.

A couple of hours south of Vitry, at Châtillon-sur-Seine, Coote introduced them to the *Trésor de Vix* – a burial mound containing the grave of a 'princess' who died 2,500 years ago and lies with her jewels in a chariot. The wheels of the chariot were carefully removed and placed at the side, as though to prevent the *Dame de Vix* from escaping back to the upper world.

It turned into a glorious autumn afternoon as they continued their drive through the champagne country, along the valley of the Seine, then the Canal de Bourgogne and finally the river Ouche, till they reached Veuvey. There they booked into the Hôtel-Restaurant de la Vallée; it could claim no more than two stars, but had a fine position overlooking the river, and the ladies were content. Leaving Coote to rest, Billa and Freda crossed the bridge to explore the village, and found it deserted – nothing to be seen but an old man and a black cat.

Coote and Billa enjoying the lunchtime ritual (Photo: Freda Berkeley).

After a frozen dinner that owed more to the microwave than the chef, Freda went upstairs for an early night, leaving Coote and Billa mulling over the events of the day with a bottle of whisky. Sitting up in bed, with Jane's notebook on her knees, Freda brought her travel diary up to date:

> *Driving along such beautiful country gives one time to reflect on so many things. I never give a thought to No 8,* and I know it's because the last years were so unbelievably awful. I often wonder whether, if I had taken Lennox away to live a quiet life at Darby House* [their house at Burton Bradstock in Dorset] *or somewhere, he* [still] *would have got Alzheimer's with all its horrors. But I expect it would have made no difference. He loved France and we had such fun driving around together here in the old days.*

* No 8 was the house in Warwick Avenue, Little Venice, London, W2, where the Berkeleys lived for the forty-three years of their marriage. On Lennox's death in 1989 Freda moved to the mansion flat in Bayswater.

III

Freda and Lennox

Half-French himself, Lennox Berkeley did indeed love France, its people and their way of life. Though born near Oxford, the son of a naval officer and a French mother, he was brought up as much in France as in England, and was bilingual. His paternal grandmother, the Dowager Countess of Berkeley, lived in Nice, where his maternal grandfather, Sir James Harris, a favourite of Queen Victoria, was British Consul. His parents were constantly on the move, but always retained a foothold in France.

At Merton College, Oxford, in the Twenties, Lennox's subjects had included French and Old French, but his immersion in music left little time for academic work, and his French reading was confined to mediaeval poetry and modern novels. While still at Oxford he met Ravel, who looked at his music, recognised its promise but deplored its lack of formal technique. To put the young man on the right path Ravel recommended a period of study with Nadia Boulanger in Paris. On leaving Oxford in the summer of 1926 Lennox went straight to Paris and to Boulanger – and immediately wondered why he had not made the move before.

Lennox was in his element in Paris. He had always known it was the place to be: money went further, attitudes were more liberal, his parents, now in Provence, were closer at hand, and the arts were seething with the new ideas of Stravinsky, Diaghilev, Cocteau, Apollinaire and Gide. The very air of Paris was an inspiration.

Perhaps it also helped that Catholicism was still a potent force in France, for Lennox had been moving towards Rome for some time, drawn largely by the beauty and the mystery of the traditional Latin liturgy. After flirting with Anglo-Catholicism at Oxford, he completed his religious journey in Paris, where he converted to Roman Catholicism in 1929. He even considered becoming a priest, but he was torn by the conflicting pressures of faith and the flesh: how to reconcile the religious life with his feelings as a homosexual, in a Church that regarded any sex outside marriage as a sin. This was a tussle that was to beset him for seventeen more years, when suddenly his life took a new turn.

After six years with Boulanger, intensively studying harmony and counterpoint, with the cantatas of Bach and the neo-classical scores of Stravinsky as paradigms, he began to look back across the Channel for performances – and recognition; in return Britain looked to him. In 1936 he was invited to represent his native country at a music festival in Barcelona. There he met and fell in love with another young English composer, Benjamin Britten. The two men agreed to live and work together, and two years later Lennox returned to England to join Britten in his converted windmill at Snape in Suffolk. But when the younger composer formed a passion for an even younger German poet, Lennox was abandoned. A few months later, partly to escape the demands of both, Britten set sail for America with Peter Pears, the man who was to share the rest of his life, and Lennox had to face the reality that his dream was over.

At the outbreak of war, Lennox, then 36, had been too old for conscription, but a year later he decided to volunteer, and his chosen service, like that of so many of his Oxford friends, was the RAF, but he was turned down because of colour blindness. He then decided to do his bit for London by working as an Air Raid Warden, and for France by joining the BBC French Service, whereupon the

War Office placed him on the list of those in Reserved Occupations who were barred from active service.

After a year or two the BBC decided he would be of even more use in the Music Department, and it was there, in 1944, that Lennox met Freda Bernstein. He was building orchestral programmes by day, and doing air-raid work by night; she was his secretary.

Orphaned at five, Freda was the only child of a Lithuanian Jewish merchant from Merthyr Tydfil and a Christian cook in Swiss Cottage. Left to the inept supervision of the Public Trustee, she was brought up by grandparents in Paddington, educated at a High Anglican boarding school in Berkshire, then sent to live with a vicar whose wife abused and beat her. At 21, she was still full of anxieties: afraid of the dark, of traffic and of being left alone. With no father or mother or siblings, Freda was lonely and looking for a husband. Lennox was 41 and living unhappily with a young airman. Both he and she were lost souls, and, in their need of reassurance and their yearning for order and quiet domesticity, they fell in love.

In the bitter winter of 1946, to their friends' astonishment, they married. Freda was attended by her landlady, Lennox by his airman. The future did not look promising, but the doubters had to eat their hats, for, against all odds, the marriage was a conspicuously happy one, producing three sons and a deluge of Lennox's best music. He had gained a beautiful and devoted wife, a family, social respectability, and the blessing of his Church. Newly confident together, they both found, for the first time, a sense of peace and fulfilment. Over the next forty years, as their three sons grew up and moved on, Lennox continued to write, his music was played widely at home and abroad, and he was showered with honours and a knighthood.

Alzheimer's crept up slowly. Walking with his old friend, the diarist James Lees-Milne, in Badminton Park in the summer of 1982, Lennox admitted that he had days when he could not write and feared he might never compose again. Afterwards Lees-Milne recorded in his diary that Lennox 'lives in a cloud'. For some time he had been working on a major commission for English National Opera – a piece about the family portraits in a country house coming back to life* – but in 1983 he had to give up, as he became increasingly confused and incoherent, unable to compose, and fretting about imaginary appointments.

His eldest son, the composer Michael Berkeley, remembers helping Lennox with his composing in those last years of trying to work – and of having to put the note-tails the right way up.

'He had always been so quietly spoken, modest and private', Michael wrote years later, 'that the descent into Alzheimer's, with its rampant invasion of privacy, seemed particularly monstrous.'

Caring for a husband with dementia was indeed 'unbelievably awful', and Freda did consider moving from the house in Little Venice which they had shared for more than forty years, but she knew that a move to new surroundings would disorientate him further. Eventually she had to take on full-time carers: it was a taxing job and very often the carers themselves required as much attention as their patient.

Lennox died on Boxing Day 1989 in a geriatric ward in St Charles' Hospital, London. 'I was strangely relieved', Michael wrote, 'that pneumonia – the old man's friend – should have released him at last, and with relative tenderness, from the tyranny of dementia.'[1]

---

* The opera, *Faldon Park*, had been suggested to him by its librettist, Winton Dean, as early as 1971.

IV

Burgundy

The coffee was so unpleasant at the hotel in Veuvey-sur-Ouche – Billa said it tasted of onions – that they did not linger over breakfast on the morning of Friday the 5th October. Instead, with the mist rising from the river to reveal the autumn colours of the trees lining the bank, they set off for Beaune, the wine capital of Burgundy, half an hour to the south.

In the collegiate church they admired the altar tapestries illustrating the life of the Virgin, but it was the mediaeval hospital which caught their imagination – in particular the rows of curtained double beds along the walls of the vast *Salle des Pôvres*. Freda thought it very cosy that the poor patients had to share a bed, but Billa was appalled and said it certainly would not have done for her. Coote pointed out, with her tongue in her cheek, that there were probably private sickrooms for the Quality.

Visiting the covered market, they bought some local produce – pieces of gamey *poulet de Bresse*, the most delicious (and most expensive) chicken in France, some Jura cheese, a bottle of Burgundy – and stopped for a picnic in the nearby village of Saint-Léger-sur-Dheune.

Pressing on for Cluny, Coote noticed a sign for Taizé and decided to make a détour to visit the ecumenical Christian monastic community founded there exactly fifty years earlier, as a place of silence and work following the defeat of France. Coote, who had been before, rested in the car while the others went into the Church of Reconciliation. Both Billa, an active Anglican, and Freda, a recently more active Catholic, were deeply impressed by the large numbers of

Salle des Pôvres, Beaune

young people sitting in silence on stools outside the church, and by the 'deep, deep silence within'.

In Cluny they had hoped to visit the Romanesque Abbey, which Freda had seen with Lennox years before, but, unlike Taizé, where tour groups were forbidden, Benedictine Cluny admitted only tour groups, and, since 'groups are anathema to us all', they turned tail and drove on through Macon to Bourg-en-Bresse, only just making it before the doors of the Royal Monastery of Brou were closed.

And what a monastery: a collection of early sixteenth-century Benedictine buildings with a spectacular Gothic church, all built or restored by Margaret, Archduchess of Austria and Regent of the Habsburg Netherlands, as a mausoleum in loving memory of her third and favourite husband, Philibert the Handsome, Duke of Savoy, who had died in 1504 after catching cold while hunting. When she herself died in 1530, she was laid to rest in an even more sumptuous tomb: on the top section, carved in marble, she is

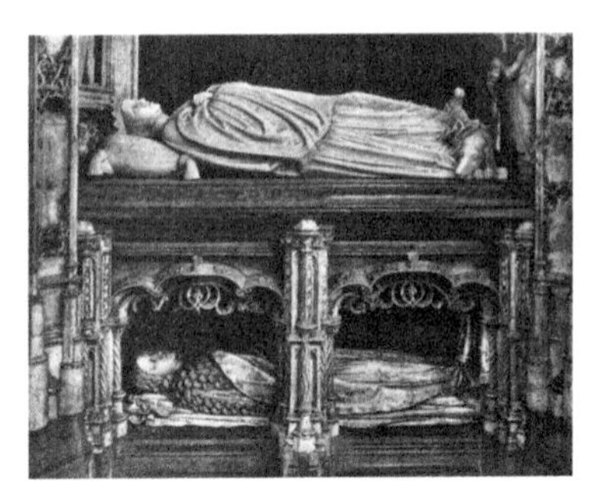

Tomb of Margaret of Austria, Monastery of Brou at Bourg-en-Bresse.

shown in all her temporal grandeur, lying under a canopy wearing a coronet and embroidered robes, her arms folded and her feet resting on a greyhound, and in the lower section, she is an alabaster corpse, her tumbling locks covering her like a mantle, her feet bare. Freda's eye for the curious did not fail to notice that the sole of the princess's left foot bears a grim representation of the gangrenous wound which killed her. Since her own infected foot was no better, and continuing to hurt, she loosened the shoe strap and limped back to the car.

Billa said she was surprised the mausoleum had escaped the vandalism of the Revolution, and Coote explained that the local people had used the church as a barn, covering the tombs with hay, and keeping livestock in the nave and the apse.

Billa and Coote priming themselves for the Simplon Tunnel (Photo: Freda Berkeley).

After a night in a modern hotel in Bourg – with baths and their best breakfast yet – they set off at seven the next morning for a long drive over the top of Lake Geneva, and what Freda's travel diary calls, perhaps with some relief, 'a no-culture day'.

> *We wanted to get through the Simplon Tunnel at lunchtime, & we did! Drove through incredibly beautiful country to get to it – mountains & waterfalls & winding roads – then our first view of Mont Blanc – the bright sun shining on a lot of snow . . . C. said she had never had a better view of it. The tunnel takes 20 mins to get through* [by car-carrying shuttle train from Brig to Iselle] *& then – Italy! A thrill after so many years away from it. I feel incredibly privileged to be doing & seeing all this with two such dear friends – & en route to Kardamyli!*

V

Piedmont and Puglia

What Freda did not record in her diary was that she suffered from claustrophobia, and had a particular horror of tunnels – in London she always used buses rather than the underground. Her companions must have dosed her up with whisky to help her through the tunnel, but there is no mention of this in the diary, just the relief of being out in the open air again, and in Italy.

Freda, fist still clenched nervously, after the Simplon Tunnel (Photo: Coote Heber-Percy).

With the dramatic alpine scenery now behind them, they drove down through the foothills to the flat lands of Piedmont, stopping by the road for their lunchtime picnic. Coote had planned to treat them to a night in the Roman town of Casale Monferrato, but they could not find a hotel, so they decided to drive on to Alessandria. First, though, they visited some baroque palaces, the Duomo and the synagogue – and sought help for Freda's sore foot.

When at last they found a *farmacista* Freda was almost more pleased that he looked like the Polish composer Witold Lutosławski than that he had made her feel so much better. His treatment involved antibiotic creams, a great deal of tender rubbing and a puttee of bandaging from toe to calf. Feeling she owed her friends a little treat for waiting, Freda gave them coffee with a plate of *krumiri*, the local boomerang-shaped egg-flour-and-butter biscuits with bitter-chocolate nuggets which melted deliciously when dunked.

After the unscheduled night in Alessandria's Hotel Lux, and a gloomy Sunday breakfast of cold boiled eggs, they set off for Parma, stopping en route to visit the flamboyant Carthusian monastery in Pavia. Billa disapproved of what she thought was an unnecessary show of extravagance by an ascetic order, but she was amused by the hippopotamus teeth decorating Baldassare's monumental triptych in the sacristy. Freda liked the terrace of 24 monks' cells built around the Great Cloister – each two storeys high, with its own little garden and a hatch by the front door so food could be delivered without anyone having to break the vow of silence.

Billa could not resist putting the Carthusian vow to the test. Calling in at the shop she asked the monk at the counter if he would be good enough to explain what herbs were used in the manufacture of the community's soaps. The young monk whispered the three herbal ingredients: 'Lavanda, camomilla e radice di marshmallow'. Billa bought a box.

In Parma that night, after checking in to the Hotel Button in the old quarter, they had a slug of whisky in Billa's bedroom, then found a local trattoria for a supper of local ingredients: prosciutto di Parma and broccoli with home-made fusilli and shavings of Parmigiano-Reggiano, then pear and chocolate cake for pudding.

Before they left Parma on Monday the 8th October, Coote was determined her friends should see the Palazzo della Pilotta on the edge of the Parma River and the treasure hidden in its Great Hall: the baroque Teatro Farnese, one of the oldest and most magnificent theatres in the world. The palazzo took a direct hit in an Allied bombing raid in May 1944, when it was mistaken for marshalling yards, as part of the RAF's systematic bombing of the European railway system. As a WAAF officer stationed in southern Italy at the time, Coote knew all about this, and years later she remembered reading that the palazzo had been rebuilt to the original design of 1618, using the original materials rescued from the site. Now

Teatro Farnese, Parma.

was her chance to see the results, and to show Billa and Freda for the first time.

The massive but plain front, rising three storeys high, over a long arcade, gives no idea of the magnificence that lies inside – or its scale. Ascending a grand staircase within the palace, the visitors entered a huge auditorium like a classical Roman stadium, sky and floating gods painted on the ceiling to give an al fresco impression. Around the edge, beneath two rows of triumphal arches surmounted by equestrian portraits of Farnese dukes, the seating (for 3,000) is arranged on steps enclosed by a balustrade, rather like the Albert Hall. The central arena was designed to be left empty for mock naval battles and horse events such as jousts and tournaments.

Some of the bomb damage has been left unrestored, as a reminder of the bombing. Billa read that the theatre was only rarely used any more, but she recognised it as the setting for the film of *Rigoletto*. It seems the director, Jean-Pierre Ponnelle, was inspired by contemporary reports of the opening performance of the Farnese in 1628 – a fantastic production of an opera-ballet called *Mercurio e Marte* (Mercury and Mars), with music by Monteverdi. According to a contemporary booklet, 'all the words were sung by the most famous musicians of Christianity'.* That first Farnese show included ballet, a display of horsemanship, and a love-interest sub-plot relating the passionate affair of the alpha-male Mars and the soft and naughty Venus. The whole thing reached a dramatic climax when the stage and arena were flooded with two feet of water for a spectacular naval battle, involving ships and shipwrecks, furies, tritons, gods and monsters. The curtain finally fell when Jupiter, king of the gods, plunged down from the sky with a retinue of a hundred attendants, and ordered peace.

After spending longer than intended at the Farnese Coote decided to take the autostrada for the 120 miles southeast to their next stop, Cesena. She hated motorway driving as a general rule, but wanted to allow plenty of time for the Malatestiana Library, before driving a further two hours, via San Marino, to Urbino for the night.

The Malatestiana is a century and a half older than the Farnese, and the visitors found it just as impressive in its cool, scholarly way. Like a church, it has a high-vaulted ceiling, a rose window at the far end and, on each side of the 'nave', 29 rows of pews and reading desks, with the oldest books chained to them, and almost as many Venetian side windows providing ample light for reading.

The library owes its existence to the Malatesta family, which ruled Rimini for two centuries. Above the walnut entrance door, in the marble pediment, is a relief sculpture of the Malatesta emblem, an elephant, long and low-slung with vast ears. Draped along its body is a banner bearing the family's cocky boast, 'Elephas Indus culices non timet' (The elephant isn't afraid of gnats).

The little city of Urbino, on the slopes of the Appenines, turned out to be as full as Casale, but eventually – and despite heavy rain – the travellers found themselves rooms in the two-star Hotel San Giovanni, in a quiet street leading down from the centre to a park

---

* The libretto by the poet and philosopher Claudio Achillini has survived, but the score is lost.

Reading Room, *Biblioteca Malatestiana*, Cesena.

enclosing a mediaeval fortress. The rooms of the hotel were small and basic but clean, and the staff friendly. Perfect, and, good value for money, as Coote was pleased to note. Freda never minded where she was, so long as she was with friends, but in her diary she observed wryly: 'Alvilde would have a fit if she saw some of the places we stay in.'

Alvilde Lees-Milne, still then alive, was a gardener-de-luxe – her clients included the Queen of Jordan and Mick Jagger. Married to the diarist James, Alvilde was notoriously censorious and interfering, listening in on other people's telephone conversations and steaming open their letters. She always insisted on the best in hotels, as in clothes, music, houses and gardens, and could be withering if her friends failed to match her standards, but they excused her captiousness as a sign of insecurity. Formerly the lover of the Singer heiress and arts patron, Winnaretta, princesse de Polignac, Alvilde used to tell Freda she owed it to Lennox to 'do something about' her hair and teeth, though both were widely admired just as they were. Nevertheless she was not ungenerous, and, to make sure that her friend passed muster, she passed on to Freda all her cast-off couturier clothes.

The next morning they visited the Ducal Palace, and the National Gallery within it. Overwhelmed by so much Renaissance magnificence, Freda felt more at home in the *Studiolo*, the tiny and exquisite inner sanctum, with its *trompe-l'oeil* shelves and benches holding life-like images of musical instruments, scores and books, caged parrots, squirrels, and distant views – all created with marquetry; above these, portraits of Illustrious Men, including Moses, Plato and Dante. The little room was designed as a place for study and contemplation – and a reminder that its noble proprietor, Federico da Montefeltro, Duke of Urbino, possessed all the learning, cultivation and virtues of the Renaissance.

From Urbino the Rover took them three hours south down the Adriatic coast to Ortona, site of one of the fiercest battles of the Second World War and home of the bones of St Thomas the apostle. They arrived in the rush-hour, in the dark, and could not see the hotel which Coote had marked in her guidebook. But Billa, bossy and bold, got out of the car outside another hotel, the Ideale, in a narrow street in the centre, and though the manager told her it was

Above: Musical instruments depicted in the Urbino *Studiolo*.

Right: Federico da Montefeltro and his son Guidobaldo (painting by Pedro Berruguete, Galleria Nazionale delle Marche).

full that night she talked him into giving them two cosy rooms – and a space for the Rover in the underground garage. Freda was full of admiration for the bulldog in Billa – and the guide dog in Coote:

Arrived here in the dark. Billa is wonderful, going into hotels, booking rooms. And Coote, against all odds, keeping her head in the rush hours, with terrific hooting behind – and me cursing & trying to follow the signs. We had 2 large whiskies on arrival.

Freda's feet were killing her. While Coote was having a shower, and Billa settling herself into her own room next door, Freda took off her shoes, climbed onto her narrow bed and fell asleep. Suddenly the door was thrown open and she woke with a start as a woman barged in, screaming. All Freda's childhood nightmares returned and, still half asleep, she imagined the woman was a witch. If she had had a Crucifix, she would have waved it aloft to ward off the power of darkness. Instead she produced her bandaged leg and waggled that as a frightful warning. The ruse worked, and the woman fled in alarm. Partly to expunge the memory of her visitation, and partly to assuage the pain in her foot, Freda swallowed a handful of Lutosławski's painkillers, and soon felt much better. She never did discover who the intruder was, or why she was screaming.

They dined that night in a fish restaurant called the Miramare, to which one of the brothers who ran the hotel had led them. It looked ghastly, Freda wrote – 'all neon lights and red paint, & full of a huge party of men like the mafiosi in Jonathan Miller's production of *Rigoletto*', but it turned out to be ideal. The three widows ordered *brodetto*, the local fish stew, which was served in large crocks, with special bibs which the young waiter draped around the ladies' necks to mop up any spillages. Afterwards they found their way back to the Ideale, and slept like logs – on firm mattresses with soft pillows and crisp linen.

Breakfast the next morning was so good, with *cornetto* pastries, chewy Pugliese bread, prosciutto, fresh fruit, yogurt and cappuccino, that they were late setting off for Day Eight.

Extraordinary to think it's a week since we left London. As Coote says, it could be seven years! Have had so much time to think, driving for miles – just what was needed.

Their destination was Barletta, with a stop in San Severo, where Coote had been stationed during the Italian Campaign of 1943–5. The airbase there was abandoned in the year the war ended, and she had always wanted to go back to see what it looked like now.

VI

Coote's war

Coote had trained for her war work in the Allied Central Interpretation Unit at RAF Medmenham in Buckinghamshire, where her logical mind, patience and natural curiosity had proved invaluable qualities in the analysis of photographs taken by reconnaissance aircraft flying over occupied Europe. The work involved the monitoring of shipping movements, and the study of photos of airfields, aircraft, marshalling yards and railways, ports and beaches; it was highly important, and top secret. The reports of the Interpreters (who included Churchill's daughter, Sarah) played their part in many decisive events of the war, including the breaching of the Ruhr dams, the sinking of the German battleship *Tirpitz*, and the D-Day landings.

In December 1943, as the Germans retreated northwards through Europe, and the Allies prepared for the European Campaign, Coote and a handful of other carefully-chosen WAAF Photographic Interpreters were flown in Mitchell bombers to San Severo, to work on site with the RAF in support of the Mediterranean Allied Photo Reconnaissance Wing at nearby Foggia. Their specific task in Italy was to interpret photographs of enemy targets before a bombing raid, and to cross-examine the crews for further information when they returned.

The airfield lay about two-and-a-half miles northeast of San Severo, on land attached to a farm called *Torre dei Giunchi* (Tower of Bulrushes, a name probably derived from the stream that runs through the farm). It had formed part of a complex of 22 military airfields around Foggia, built by the Italian Royal Air Force before

Left: 683 Squadron RAF. Right: RAF Supermarine Spitfire, Foggia, 1944 (asisbiz.com)

the war. In September 1943 the Luftwaffe had seized the complex, but as the Allies moved into mainland Italy, the British Eighth Army had captured the Foggia airfields for the support of strategic bombing, escort and reconnaissance missions and tactical fighter operations.

Like the other bases in the complex, San Severo airfield was essentially temporary, consisting of grass and pierced-steel-planking runways, with hardstand parking, blister hangars and a steel control tower. The air crews based there from October 1943 were squadrons from the RAF and the South African Air Force, fresh from the Desert Campaign in North Africa,* and reconnaissance and fighter units of the United States Air Force. Initially the RAF used de Havilland Mosquito aircraft, but in September 1944 these were replaced by Supermarine Spitfires, camouflaged blue. The target areas in their huge parish were Northern Italy, Southeast France, Austria, Germany, Czechoslovakia, Poland, and the Balkans. The aircraft carried no radio and no armaments and flew unescorted, so they had to maintain a height of 40,000 feet over

* In the Spring of 1944 a South African Air Force pilot returned from a mission over German-held southern Poland with the first grim evidence of the Nazi concentration camps. He had been sent to photograph a rubber factory near the town of Oświęcim (soon to become notorious as Auschwitz), and when the photos were analysed the Interpreters found fortified walls, barbed wire, gallows, gas chambers, cremation chimneys and rows of prisoners. See the account of the work of 60 Squadron SAAF online at http://www.saairforce.co.za/the-airforce/squadrons/12/60-squadron

enemy territory, to reduce the chance of engagements. Their missions often lasted many hours, and involved flying through intense and accurate flak. If an aircraft ever did encounter enemy fire the instruction was to turn and run for home: it was better, their superiors thought, to return alive with some photographs than not to return at all.

The Spitfires carried their cameras in a special compartment behind the pilot, who operated them by remote control. On reaching his target, the pilot would switch on the cameras and make a series of runs, taking overlapping photographs for stereoscopic examination later. The moment the aircraft returned to base, the films were removed from the cameras and rushed to the photo lab for developing. The negatives were then printed and delivered to the Photographic Interpreter teams who worked through the night, analysing the photographs and cross-examining the crews. What Coote and her colleagues were trained to look for was evidence of damage caused by Allied bombing raids, in order to provide tactical intelligence for the forces advancing to those points.[2]

With the Germans now in retreat, life at the airfield was comparatively peaceful – until a tragic accident in the summer of 1944. Before abandoning San Severo the previous summer the Luftwaffe had dumped their unused munitions near the airfield, presumably hoping they would explode and blow the place up. RAF bomb disposal teams had been trying to make the devices safe ever since the Allies arrived in the autumn of 1943. But the following July there was a huge explosion: ten thousand shells, mines and bombs were scattered over an area of about 20 acres – and seven airmen were killed. Many of the surviving missiles were even more dangerous now, but in view of the threat they posed to the lives of all the service personnel on the airfield, demolition work had to be done immediately and with extreme caution. The work started on 11 August, and by the 18th the RAF bomb disposal team had defused everything and the area was declared safe again. Coote was in

Coote Lygon with the RAF Night Photography Section at San Severo, 1944.

San Severo throughout all this, and knew the officer commanding the bomb disposal operation, but she never spoke about it afterwards.*

The RAF personnel at the San Severo airfield were billeted in six-man tents, lined up in rows with the orderly room and the mess hall at one end. Lighting was provided by a dim light bulb at the centre of each tent, and the floor was bare grass, soon trodden into mud. The WAAF officers lived and messed in a nearby block of flats. The food was awful, Coote said, because the Italian cook was selling off their rations. Sleeping and washing arrangements were basic. There was no hot water and the bathroom was full of cockroaches. They slept on newspapers spread out on camp beds, and for extra warmth in winter they borrowed woollen vests from the pilots to wear under their pyjamas.

Coote enjoyed life in the WAAF at San Severo, and after the war she used to entertain her friends with RAF yarns. She had a good ear for language and especially for the colourful slang of the pilots, with which, between puffs on her cigar, she peppered her

* For his part in the San Severo bomb disposal operation, Acting Squadron Leader Frederick Charles Batten, R. A. F. V. R., was awarded the O. B. E. (Military Division) – *London Gazette*, 3 July 1945.

stories. Paddy Leigh Fermor, who relished Coote's tales, was inspired to write a poem based on them:

'What's happened to Winko?' asked Groupie.
The Mess Corporal wagged his old head:
'He said that he'd fancy a Bass, sir,
But he went for a Burton instead.'[3]

VII

San Severo

Avoiding the tolls on the busy Autostrada Adriatica, Coote drove the Rover gently southeast down the coast on the Strada Statale 16. Twenty minutes after passing the fishing town of Termoli, the road turned inland over the Foggian plain to San Severo. The airfield used to lie two-and-a-half miles northeast of the city, but that was forty-five years ago: since then the city had grown and spread, and the new Autostrada Adriatica from Bologna to Taranto now connected San Severo to the coast and to Foggia – possibly right over what used to be the airfield. But Coote was determined to find it, and, as a map expert, she knew where to look.

Leaving the highway just before the turn-off to the city, she joined the ring road heading east. To the left and right were vineyards, olive groves and wheat fields as far as the eye could see. As she approached the bridge over the autostrada she felt she was getting warm, and, as the car dipped down the other side, an instinct told her to take the minor road immediately to the right, which ran beside the autrostrada in the direction of San Severo. She drove for a minute or two, past a ploughed field and then a vast olive grove, and then she saw it: through a gate, up a track, the ruins of an old tufa-block building which she recognised as a wartime photo lab. With this landmark she now knew exactly where they were, and could place the entire airfield.

Reversing into the gateway, she drove back up to the ring road, turned right into Strada Serpente and right again, through gates, into the *Masseria Torre dei Giunchi*. This farm and its outbuildings had formed the American end of the airfield, where the pilots of the 31st Fighter Group and their P-51 Mustang fighter planes were based, off-limits to WAAFs, and even now, all these years later, Coote drove a little hesitantly, half-expecting to be challenged.

Parking outside a building which she remembered as having been used by the U.S. Army Information Service, Coote got out and went over to a group of men talking by an open door. Emerging from an English car and looking unmistakably English, she surprised them by speaking fluent Italian. She explained who she was, that she had been based here in the war, and one of the men took his cap off. She asked if she could drive her friends around. They said there was nothing to see, but she was welcome to take a look.

There was no sign of runways or hangars or any sort of military construction, just farm buildings, tractors, machinery and cars, and beyond them, acres of ploughed fields, divided not by hedges or fences but only by access tracks. Coote pointed out where things used to be, but she guessed it was not terribly interesting for her friends, so she drove on to San Severo.

Finding a place to park in the centre, she took them to see the building she remembered best: the *Teatro Comunale*, a neoclassical opera house which stands in the grounds of a thirteenth-century

Left: San Severo coat of arms.

Right: Teatro Verdi, San Severo.

Benedictine convent. The theatre was built under the influence of the Mussolini Government in 1937, in the spirit of Fascist triumphalism, so it is nothing if not grand, both inside and out.

Finding the theatre closed, they settled themselves outside a trattoria further down the street, where they could admire the baroque entrance of the Benedictine convent, which is now the local courthouse. But Coote's mind was still on the theatre, and, over a bottle of sparkling San Severo *Bombino Bianco*, she recalled the club which the officers at the airbase formed in one of the theatre's salons. For an hour or two in the evenings they used to gather there to forget the war. Sometimes there was dancing – to the music of a horn gramophone, or, if they were lucky, a live band – and she would think of the riotous dances at Madresfield and wonder if those days were gone for ever.

The ladies ordered a simple Pugliese lunch of *pancotto* (a soup made with a brew of local herbs, stale bread, potatoes and tomatoes), followed by baked aubergines stuffed with breadcrumbs, capers, eggs, cheese, olive oil and basil. Come coffee, Coote continued to reminisce – this time about someone Billa knew too.

She said that while she was at San Severo in July 1944 – at the time the Nazi munitions dump exploded – she received a telegram from her old friend Evelyn Waugh, then a captain in the Royal Marines, to say he had been hurt in an air crash in Yugoslavia and was undergoing treatment for burns in the nearby town of Bari (another part of the Foggia airfields complex). He and Churchill's son, Randolph, had been on their way from their headquarters in Bari to the Croatian island of Vis, on a secret mission to support Marshal Tito's partisans. After lunching with Tito in Vis they were flying on for further secret talks when their aircraft crashed during a night-time landing in

Evelyn Waugh and Randolph Churchill, Croatia, 1944.

the spa town of Topusko. Of the nineteen people on board, ten were killed, but both Waugh and Churchill survived and were flown back to the military hospital in Bari.

When Coote visited them there, some time after 18 July, they were still bandaged like mummies – and, according to another friend who saw them at much the same time, they were arguing about nothing in particular and shouting at each other.[4] Coote said Waugh's hands were so badly burned that he could not hold a pen, and Churchill was 'creating a fine fuss' in a neighbouring bed.[5] Waugh had just finished writing *Brideshead Revisited* and was expecting the proofs to be air-dropped in at any moment. In a letter the previous year he had written to tell her he was writing 'a very beautiful book, to bring tears, about very rich, beautiful, high-born people who live in palaces and have no troubles except what they make themselves, and those are mainly the demons, sex and drink'.[6] It was an ironic résumé intended to parody the kind of reaction he distinctly hoped the book would not receive. Coote had understood this, but may not have known then that the book was inspired by Waugh's rackety life at Oxford and in particular by his friendship with her family.

In the Bari hospital he told her more. The new book, he said, was 'all about a family whose father lives abroad, as it might be Boom [Coote's father, Lord Beauchamp] – but it's not Boom – and a younger son: people will say he's like Hughie [Coote's brother] but you'll see he's not really Hughie – and there's a house as it might be Mad [Madresfield], but it isn't really Mad.' From all these uncertain negatives Coote deduced that *Brideshead Revisited* probably was based on the Lygons and Madresfield, and she must have had misgivings. But she bit them back, and always maintained that the Lygons were only partly the inspiration.*

* Philip Eade's biography of Waugh argues that the character who became the book's hero, Sebastian Flyte, was indeed 'not really Hughie' but Waugh's Oxford love, Alastair Graham.

VIII

Madresfield

Coote's childhood and early life at Madresfield were tempestuous and sad but far from lonely. She was 18 when her father, the 7th Earl Beauchamp, leader of the Liberal Party in the House of Lords, was denounced as a homosexual and hounded out of the country, leaving the family shocked, ostracised and permanently fractured. Exposed by his bullying brother-in-law – Bend'Or, Duke of Westminster – Lord Beauchamp was visited one summer's evening in 1931 by a grim deputation of three fellow Knights of the Garter. The King, they told him, had been informed of allegations against him, involving criminal acts of indecency with other men. To prevent embarrassing the court and perhaps precipitating a political crisis, he was required to leave England by midnight. 'Dear Bugger-in-Law,' wrote Bend'Or a little later, 'You got what you deserved. Yours, Westminster.'

Coote's mother, though innocent of the details, had long suspected that her husband's desires 'ran contrary to what is natural', but the news of his banishment brought on a nervous breakdown and she took to her bed in Bend'Or's house in Cheshire – and remained in his thrall for the rest of her life. But Coote and most of her siblings stood by their father, supporting him in every way, and refusing to testify against him, though they all knew of his affairs with his handsome young footmen, and used to warn any male friends who came to stay that they should take care to lock their doors at night.

The Lygon children had never liked their mother, but all, except the heir, William, Lord Elmley, adored their father. According to

Lord Beauchamp's biographer, Jane Mulvagh, they were in constant fear that he would take his life after the scandal broke, 'so they decided that at all times one of them should watch over him. A dutiful rota began as the older children took their turn – week in week out, in Europe and further afield – by their father's side.'[7] For the remaining seven years of his life he wandered sadly from Paris to Sydney to San Francisco and finally to New York, whiling away his time embroidering cushions.

When their father left England in June 1931, the two eldest sons, William (later to be re-born as 'Bridey' in *Brideshead Revisited*) and the exquisite Hugh (the novel's teddy-bear-hugging 'Sebastian') took over Madresfield's 162 rooms with their three unmarried sisters, including Coote. This may have been the year of the banking crisis which ushered in the Great Depression, but at Madresfield the age of the Bright Young Things was still in full swing. With no parents to watch over them, armies of servants to look after them, cars and horses to carry them wherever they wanted to go, and their own bank accounts to draw on, the Lygon siblings were able to do as they liked, and they did – though Lord Beauchamp's habit of morning prayers continued in the Chapel, with Coote playing the organ. Protected by double moats, Madresfield became notorious for its wild parties. Nor were the frolics confined to Worcestershire: the young Lygons' London base – Halkyn House in Belgrave Square – was no less of a Liberty Hall (today it's the Ghanaian High Commission).

At Christmas 1931 William and Hugh invited the unruly Evelyn Waugh to join the fun – they had been intimates at Oxford, moving in the same circle of homosexual drinking parties. For Waugh, then broke and homeless after his divorce, the rich and aristocratic Lygons opened up a glamorous new world, and he fell in love with the entire family. For the lost Lygons, the puckish Waugh was a welcome diversion from their troubles. He wrote them smutty letters full of private jokes and accounts of orgies, and once, on

Lygons, 1925 (Coote, Maimie, Sibell, Lettice, Lady Beauchamp, Lord Beauchamp, William, Hugh, Dickie).

Maimie, Waugh and Coote.

finding Coote's diary, he embellished her innocent drawing of a carthorse with a huge penis.

It was during this time that Waugh wrote his third novel, *Black Mischief*, and dedicated it to sweet-natured Coote and her blonde older sister, Mary ('Maimie'), who inspired the character of *Brideshead*'s Julia Flyte.* Coote remembered Waugh 'groaning loudly as he shut himself away' at Madresfield to concentrate on his writing. Jane Mulvagh has observed that 'Waugh relaxed amidst the sisters' silliness, mimicry and informality, and delighted in their childlike world of games, secret language and gentle teasing. They became his adoring audience'.[8]

Coote had already met Billa Harrod and Joan Eyres Monsell by then. They had all reached the age of eighteen the previous year, 1930, and had come out as debutantes in the same Season.

Billa was short and shapely, dark-haired and fun, and had just completed a brief period of study at the Sorbonne. Joan was tall and fair, rich and beautiful, the polished product of finishing schools in Paris and Florence, and the darling of the society columns. Her

---

* Maimie later married a Russian prince, but after their divorce in 1957 she had a mental breakdown and devoted the rest of her life to her Pekingeses and the bottle. She died in 1982.

father – then Sir Bolton Eyres Monsell, later Viscount Monsell – was a Conservative politician who rose to become First Lord of the Admiralty. Her mother, Sybil née Eyres, was an heiress who inherited a cotton fortune. Both Joan and Billa had made their mark as (highbrow) It Girls, but kind Coote, with her specs, her big feet and her embonpoint, was no sexpot and suffered from the further handicap of the family scandal. She was, however, a sport, and threw herself into a deb's life as though it were a game of charades.

Presentation at court was a major performance, and involved some complicated dressing-up. Sponsored by older ladies who had themselves been debs, the three friends were shown how to climb into short-sleeved white dresses with *décolletés plongeants*, how to pull on white gloves beyond the elbows, how to swish their long trains, and how to attach veils to their hair with the three white ostrich feathers prescribed by court protocol. Thus identically robed each of the young women had to make a ceremonial entrance into the Throne Room at Buckingham Palace. There, before the assembled court, they were required to step forward in their light pumps and perform two deep curtsies – one to King George V, the other to Queen Mary – before reversing from the royal presence, while trying not to trip over their trains. Etiquette forbade their looking directly at the monarch or his consort as they sank to the floor with eyes demurely downcast, but a discreet glance was allowed on the slow return to vertical.

Following the formal presentation, the debs faced a taxing Season of tea parties and dances, polo matches and Royal Ascot. The purpose was to display themselves – and their plunging necklines – to eligible bachelors and their mothers, with a view to making a good marriage. Coote, Billa and Joan, rebels all, went through the motions, but each was to find a husband in her own way and her own time.

As a deb Coote lived it up with Billa and Joan, serving as a sort of aide-de-camp to her dazzling sister, Maimie, escorting her to all the parties. Joan's at Dumbleton Hall in the Cotswolds were every bit as riotous as those at Madresfield. In 1936, while her parents were at the Berlin Olympics, meeting Hitler, Joan gave a party that lasted the whole weekend. Among the guests were Lord Berners and Frederick Ashton. According to Joan's biographer, Simon Fenwick, 'Everyone got drunk and a lot of clothes got flung about. Billa swung from a chandelier while performing a striptease. Years later she told a friend, 'I was starkers, my dear, absolutely starkers.'[9]

After the war Coote took up farming and riding in Gloucestershire, and was one of the last women in England to hunt side-saddle. For a time she worked as a social secretary at the British Embassy in Athens, later teaching in the city, and in 1956 she spent six months as a governess in Istanbul where she was obliged to sleep under a table. By then Joan was living with Paddy on the Greek island of Hydra, and after Istanbul Coote went to live on Hydra too. In the 1960s she returned home to England to look for a job, and placed a typically no-nonsense advertisement in a magazine, 'Woman', it said, 'wants work'. In due course she found work as an archivist at Christie's, first in the books department, then in Old Masters; during much of this time she lived on a houseboat at Chelsea Reach.

In the late 1970s she settled in Faringdon, near the Palladian big house (with its painted pigeons) which had been inherited by Robert Heber-Percy when his lover, Lord Berners, died in 1950. To general astonishment Robert asked Coote to marry him in 1985,

Left: Faringdon House. Right: Robert Heber-Percy.

possibly as an act of kindness to a penniless old friend, possibly as a joke. All but jumping for joy, Coote accepted, innocently assuming that even now, so late, and despite all evidence to the contrary, it would be a *mariage d'amour*. But it very soon became clear that it was to be as *blanc* as her trousseau. Robert's cronies resented the squire's new arrangements, and the housekeeper walked out. Within a year Coote was back in her cottage, and the following year Robert died, leaving Faringdon to his daughter by an earlier failed marriage,* and leaving Coote in Lime Tree Cottage, with her pictures by John Craxton, her signed first editions of Waugh – and little else but a ring on her finger.

* Robert Heber-Percy married Jennifer Fry in 1942, and their daughter, Victoria, was born the following year. Victoria Heber-Percy married Peter Zinovieff, and their eldest child, Sofka, who inherited the entire Faringdon estate in 1987, tells the story of the house and her grandparents in *The Mad Boy, Lord Berners, My Grandmother and Me*, Jonathan Cape, 2014.

IX

Greece

'South Italy has been ruined', wrote Freda in dismay, as they drove further south, down the coast, after San Severo, 'it's all high-rise flats and motorways'. But the ancient city of Barletta cheered them up. It was like stepping back in time, with old women on balconies chatting through the washing and flowerpots to other old women on matching balconies across the street; Vespas everywhere. There was no time to see the castle, the basilica, the opera house, but they could not miss, if only through the windows of their hotel in the Corso Vittorio Emanuele, the Colossus of Barletta, the huge bronze statue of a bearded Roman emperor washed ashore when a Venetian ship sank on its way back from the sack of Constantinople. Billa said he looked like Paddy.

Leaving Barletta early on Thursday the 11th, they sped past Bari to Brindisi, determined to board the night ferry without having to stop in the port city which had such bad memories for Coote. In 1977 when she was driving Paddy and Joan to Greece with a carload of things for Kardamyli they stopped for supper at a trattoria, and while they were eating, the car was stolen. It was later found abandoned on a rubbish tip, but everything in it and on it had gone, bar a few socks and letters. The car, however, still worked, so they were at least able to reach the Mani.[10] This time Coote was taking no risks and made her friends stay in the car till it was time to catch the Fragline ferry *Ouranos* to Greece, where they arrived safely early the next morning, as Freda's diary records:

Shared a cabin with Coote, & Billa had the one next door. Something wrong with our heating and we nearly passed out – it was so, so hot. Landed at Igoumenitsa [at 5.30 a.m.] *after a very calm voyage.*

On wheels again they drove down the coast of the Ionian Sea, stopping for a picnic in an orchard, under a tree which rained walnuts on their heads. It was a long but pleasing drive south, with the sea on one side and, on the other side, mountains covered in spruces. At the village of Nea Thesi the road turned sharply east across fertile plains to the Byzantine town of Arta. Once there they checked in to a tourist hotel, known to both Coote and Billa, who had stayed there before. And, for the first time in the nine days since they left London, Billa and Freda washed their hair, while Coote telephoned Paddy and Joan to say they had arrived in Greece and should be at Kardamyli in two days.

It was so warm this far south that they were able to dine outside, celebrating their arrival on Greek soil with ouzo, *spanakopitakia* – spinach and feta in filo pastry triangles – and lamb *kleftiko*. Then, gathering up their walking sticks, they took a little promenade before bed. Freda and Coote shared a double room, as usual, and Billa, in the absence of a spare separate room, slept under the stars on their balcony. It had been a long day, and even Billa slept soundly.

The next morning, Saturday the 13th October, they set off for Olympia: a long, hot drive for Coote. After stopping for a picnic in an olive grove, all too close to the rotting corpse of a golden jackal, they left mainland Greece at Antirrion and crossed the Gulf of Corinth by ferry to the Peloponnese peninsula. From there the road took them past Patras and around the coast to Olympia.

Warned that it was local election weekend and that everyone would have returned home to vote, they expected the hotels to be full, but found themselves rooms in a pleasant, modern hotel near the Altis, the sacred core of Ancient Olympia. Leaving Coote to rest,

Right: the Colossus of Barletta.

Below: the ferry to Greece.

Freda and Billa set off on foot to find a taverna, where, later, the trio dined on *kolokythokeftedes* (courgette patties) with cooling tzatziki, followed by seared *barbounia* (red mullet) with rice and a Greek salad.

On the Sunday morning, before the sun got even hotter, Freda and Billa checked out early to look at the ruins. The route was simple but they took a wrong turn and ended up in an olive grove, surrounded by reed beds. Fortunately Coote happened to be driving past, on her way to the Archaeological Museum, and was able to rescue them. Did they realise, she said, that they were close to the spot where the virginal nymph Syrinx, pursued by the lusty shepherd Pan, had turned herself into hollow water reeds to avoid his advances. When Pan bent over the reeds to kiss them he found that his breath produced music – and so the pan flute or *syrinx* was born. Freda was reminded not only of Debussy's *Syrinx* for solo flute, but also of the work by Poulenc which is often played as a companion piece, *Un joueur de flûte berce les ruines* (A flautist plays a lullaby for the ruins) – and of Poulenc's *Flute Sonata* which Lennox had orchestrated so successfully.

In the tourist shop Freda bought a recording of the pan flute, and, her glance falling on some souvenirs, a string of amber worry beads – the beads to amuse her assistant, Jane, back in London, amber in honour of her immigrant father, who had begun his new life in the Welsh valleys as a tinker selling trinkets from his native Lithuania.

After an early picnic they embarked on the last leg of their journey, a two-and-a-half-hour drive south, down the coast by the E55 via Kalo Nero, where the main road turned inland to Tsakona, and Kalamata, still devastated by the earthquake of 1986, then on by a twisty minor road to Kardamyli.

As their car reached the top of the mountain road, just after the village of Stavropigio, they saw beneath them a spectacular panorama radiating from the mediaeval tower houses of Kardamyli, set at the foot of Mount Taygetus, to the tip of the Deep Mani, Cape Matapan, the southernmost point of continental Europe.

Coote stopped briefly for the eagle's view, then pressed on down the mountain road to the coast. She knew that, though they were now so close, she would have to drive really slowly and take especial care because the descent was perilous, with its sharp bends, vertiginous drops, tractors, animals and crazy Greek drivers.

At last they were down on the coastal plain, and soon bumping along the cobbled lanes of Kardamyli, between mulberry trees and jasmine. A few minutes later, Coote left the Areopolis road and took a right turn down a mule track leading to the hamlet of Kalamitsi in a pebbly cove, and then another right turn, climbing up the side of a promontory, along a rough dirt track lined with cypresses, pines and olives. At the top stood the low stone house, with pale blue shutters and a terracotta-tiled roof – the hideaway which Paddy and Joan had built for themselves a quarter of a century earlier. It looked like a cross between a farmhouse, a monastery and a fortress – just the sort of place where you might expect to find a scholar-soldier and his muse.

Kalamitsi beach with the Leigh Fermors' villa overlooking it, on a headland above a small bay hidden beyond the tip of the beach.

X

Joan and Billa

Joan and Billa found husbands a great deal sooner than Coote, but both explored bumpy side-roads on the way, for neither was quite the sort of daughter her mother would have wished for.[11] Billa was sharing a flat in Holborn with her sister, and working, first, as a wardrobe mistress in films, and then, in 1937, as Secretary of the newly-formed Georgian Group, campaigning for the preservation of Georgian buildings and gardens. For a born agitator, the campaigning part came naturally; the preservation part sowed the seeds of her lifelong passion for the rescue of old buildings.

Through Joan's pianist brother, Graham, she and Billa met two of his brilliant, bisexual friends: the sleek Alan Pryce Jones, who sometimes wore make-up, and the tousled John Betjeman, who rarely brushed his teeth. By 1930 all three young men had just left Oxford under various clouds. Graham was now studying music in Paris, to the disgust of his father who considered music an unmanly profession for a gentleman; Alan was working on *The London Mercury*; and John was assistant editor of *The Architectural Review*. Alan, who was probably Graham's lover, fell instantly in love with Joan ('a lovely boy-girl ... like a ... decadent Eton athlete'),[12] and John, though engaged to Penelope Chetwode, fell for Billa ('my Turkish Delight').

The prospective fathers-in-law huffed and puffed. Penelope's father, Field Marshal Lord Chetwode, Commander-in-Chief, India, had hoped for a suitor with at least a pheasant shoot – instead his wayward daughter had found herself 'a little middle-class Dutchman'. Joan's tyrannical father, Sir Bolton Eyres Monsell, Chief

Above: Alan Pryce-Jones, Paris, 1931 (Photo: Horst P. Horst).

Right: John Betjeman, posing at Dumbleton, 1933 (Photo: Joan Eyres Monsell).

Far right: Joan Eyres Monsell.

Whip of the Conservative Party,* put Alan through a gruelling cross-examination, and, discovering that he possessed neither money nor place, told him to 'come back in a few years' time, when you have something behind you'.[13]

* He was created Viscount Monsell in 1935, married again after the death of Joan's mother, and died in 1969.

Their relative poverty, lack of country seats, and poor performance at Oxford were not all that worked against the young men. All three were, to a greater or lesser degree, homosexual. Their bohemian girlfriends knew the score and did not mind a bit. When John learned that Alan was engaged to Joan, he offered some friendly advice:

> *. . . there is one thing you must do before you marry – you must explain that you were once inverted. She won't mind at all. In fact she obviously knows as she is quite aware that old Graham and I and all our friends are inverted . . . Actually inversion is an additional charm. It worked very well with Philth* [Penelope Chetwode].[14]

If coming out as an 'invert' worked as successfully with Joan as it had with Penelope, it seems to have won the day with Billa too. Overwhelmed by Billa's 'extraordinary clothes and that loud voice and that white and painted face',[15] John Betjeman proposed marriage and Billa promptly accepted (despite her beau's hair, which looked, she said, 'like last year's nest').[16] But the affair was short-lived. Hearing rumours of the engagement, Penelope raced home from India, plucked John back from Billa, reclaimed him as her own and married him in July 1933.

Joan's affair with Alan Pryce Jones lasted much longer. At the outset she may have seen it as an escape from the restrictions of home, but as two years and more rolled by she seems to have become deeply involved, certainly more so than he. In 1932 she engineered the announcement of their engagement in the *Daily Express* but her furious father published a retraction the next day. At all events when, a little later, Alan met the French-Jewish heiress Thérèse ('Poppy') Fould-Springer (who looked a bit like Billa), he proposed to her, and refused to see Joan till he had safely placed a ring on Poppy's finger in the autumn of 1934.

Just before Christmas Joan and Alan did meet again, without

Poppy, at a party given by Joan's lifelong admirer, Cyril Connolly, with a host of literati including Evelyn Waugh, Patrick Balfour (soon to succeed his father as Lord Kinross), Henry Yorke (aka Green) and David 'Bunny' Garnett. Joan may have lost Alan but she had gained all his friends. One of them was a brilliant Oxford don, Roy Harrod, who had been an intimate of Waugh and of Coote's brother, Hugh, at Oxford (where they all belonged to the louche and boozy Hypocrites' Club, crucible of the Oxford aesthetes, whose members were permitted to 'prance but not dance' – and occasionally bit one another when drunk).[17]

Like Joan, Billa loved the company of artists and intellectuals, and was happily drawn into the homosexual web of Eton and Oxford. Joan used the word 'queer' to describe these new friends, who included Mark Ogilvie-Grant, Maurice Bowra, Patrick Balfour, Tom Driberg, Robert Byron, Eddie Gathorne-Hardy and Roy Harrod; Billa, for all her liberal views, used another word, drawing with a finger on Alan Pryce Jones's dirty car the message, 'Alan is a pansy'. According to his son, Alan took this as a tease and not a judgement. Whatever it was, it did not prevent Billa falling in love with Roy Harrod; nor did the fact that Roy was a Liberal and she a fierce and feudalistic Tory. In 1938 they married and settled in

Railway Club at Oxford (Harrod back 2nd l), Hugh Lygon (middle row 2nd left).

Roy Harrod, 1935 (by his mother, Frances Harrod; painting at Christ Church, University of Oxford).

Oxford, where Roy was Fellow in Modern History and Economics at Christ Church. He remained there till 1967 when he and Billa retired to Norfolk.*

Joan had always been interested in photography and, encouraged by John Betjeman, she took pictures of landscapes and buildings as well as of friends. Some of her photographs were published in *The Architectural Review* and *Horizon*, and when war broke out she was commissioned to photograph historic sites thought likely to be bombed. Meanwhile she had met, and, in 1939, married John Rayner, features editor of the *Daily Express*. But they fell out over their different interpretations of an open marriage, Joan taking the freer view of 'open', and the relationship soon foundered. To get away Joan took a wartime training course in encryption, and was posted as a cypher clerk to the British Embassies in, successively, Algiers, Madrid, and Cairo. It was while she was in Cairo in 1944 – living in a 'crumbling Mamaluke palace',[18] with Eddie Gathorne-Hardy and Patrick Balfour – that she met Patrick Leigh Fermor, by then a glamorous war hero.

Commissioned in the Intelligence Corps at the outset of the war, Paddy had been sent as a liaison officer to the Greeks fighting the Italians in Albania. After joining the Special Operations Executive he was parachuted into Crete during the Nazi occupation, with the task of organizing the guerilla resistance, while living as a shepherd in mountain caves. In April 1944 he and Captain William Stanley ('Bill') Moss led a team of Cretan resistance fighters in one of the most daring operations of the war. Disguised as German military policemen, the two men ambushed the staff car of the German commander, General Heinrich Kreipe, bundled him into the back, and, impersonating him and his chauffeur, they drove through

* During the war, Roy Harrod was briefly in Churchill's 'S-branch', a statistical section within the Admiralty. In the General Election of 1945 he stood as a Liberal candidate for Harrogate, but lost. Today he is best known for his biography of his friend and colleague, John Maynard Keynes, and his *International Economics*, once a standard textbook. He died in 1978.

Right: William Stanley Moss and Patrick Leigh Fermor, dressed in the stolen uniforms of German military police, Crete, 1944.

Far right: Patrick Leigh Fermor as a Major in the parachute regiment, 1945.

22 checkpoints into the mountains. For the next three weeks, hunted by German patrols, they marched the general over the mountains to a beach on the south side of the island, where they were rescued by a British motor launch and ferried to the safety of British-held Cairo. After interrogation there, Kreipe was sent to a POW camp in Canada.*

In Cairo Paddy and Bill settled in a grand villa with a ballroom in which they entertained the expatriate community, Paddy under the nickname of Lord Rakehell, Bill Moss as Mr Jack Jargon, and their SOE comrade Major Xan Fielding as Lord Hughe Devildrive. Paddy and Joan, adventurers both, were bound to meet and fall in love – and so they did, at a party at Christmas 1944. Despite affairs on both sides – his often financed by her – they remained together for the rest of her life, but they did not marry till 1968, the year the house at Kardamyli was finished.

* Later General Kreipe was transferred to a special camp in Wales, and finally released from British captivity in 1947. He died in Germany in 1976. In 1950 Moss published an account of the operation, under the title *Ill Met By Moonlight: The Abduction of General Kreipe,* which was later made into a film starring Dirk Bogarde as Leigh Fermor.

XI

Kardamyli

The three ladies had reached their journey's end, two thousand miles and eleven days from Bayswater. Coote and Billa knew the house well, yet each time they came back it cast its spell anew. The magic was an alchemy of place – on the tip of a headland over the sea; of scents – jasmine, oregano, pine; of colour – the peach flush of the Taygetus limestone; and of spirit – peace, comfort, sanctuary and, above all, the palpable presence of the hearts and minds that created it.

Coote parked the car, and they all climbed stiffly out, fumbling for their sticks, and breathing in the soft sea air of a warm October evening. Billa called hello, raising her voice over the thrum of the cicadas, but the slamming of car doors had already signalled their arrival, and, as they followed a cobbled path to the open door and entered the arcaded courtyard, picking their way over sleeping cats, Paddy sprang forward to greet them. Fit and handsome, his still-dark wavy hair immaculately brushed, he embraced his friends, making a great pretence that their appearance was a wonderful surprise. It was not really a surprise at all for it had been planned in the summer when he and Coote and Billa had met at a party given by the Devonshires at Chatsworth (and stayed up till 4.30 in the morning, as they used to at Madresfield and Dumbleton half a century earlier).[19] Soon Joan appeared, tall and straight-backed, lean and attractive, in an indigo shirt over white slacks with espadrilles, and, after further hugs, amid a babble of excited voices, she and Paddy led the visitors into the cool of the house. Paddy offered ouzo but Joan knew that what they needed after the long hot drive was a pot of tea.

The Patrick and Joan Leigh Fermor House (Photo: The Benaki Museum, Athens).

When the visitors had unpacked, rested and changed, they gathered in the great central living room – books everywhere, landscapes by Niko Ghika on the walls, colourful kilims on the stone floor – while Joan prepared a simple supper. A superb and imaginative cook, she brought them a special delicacy to nibble with their ouzo: crispbreads spread with a buttery paté she had made from the roe of sea urchins gathered on the pebbly beach below.

Paddy asked about the journey, a drive he and Joan had so often done before them – sometimes with them – and expressed relief that they had survived the perils of Brindisi. They talked of sights, towns and restaurants they all knew, of the statue in Barletta that looked so like Paddy, and of the visit to the site of the San Severo air base (which provoked, as Coote had hoped, a performance of Paddy's RAF poem).

They also talked about Alzheimer's Disease and the trials of caring for the victims – Freda spoke about Lennox's decline, and Joan spoke of the disintegration of her brother, Graham, who was now living with carers at home at Dumbleton.* Billa brought up the subject of the television film which Melvyn Bragg had made about Paddy the previous year. She made it clear that she did not approve, though she had been glad to see Paddy, and his great friend and

* Graham Eyres-Monsell, 2nd Viscount Monsell, served in the Intelligence Corps during the Second World War, reaching the rank of Lieutenant-Colonel. He died in December 1993.

Cretan comrade, Xan Fielding.* Joan broke the sad news from Spain that Xan had just been diagnosed with cancer, and would be moving to Paris for treatment.†

Billa waited till after supper to deliver her royal message. She had seen the Prince of Wales who had told her he was planning a house-party at Sandringham in April, and had asked her to try to persuade Paddy to come over for it. The prince longed to know Paddy, and Billa thought Paddy would love Sandringham, though she was not so sure that Joan would – and anyway the prince did not usually invite couples.‡ It was such fun staying at Sandringham, she said – not as ravishing as Chatsworth, but very comfortable and relaxing, with delicious food and drink.[20]

They were all such close and understanding friends that no one raised the vexed question of Paddy's 'volume three': the final instalment of his great work recounting his youthful walk through Central and Eastern Europe in the early 1930s. The second volume, *Between the Woods and the Water*, published in 1984, had ended with the words, 'TO BE CONCLUDED'. But the conclusion still had not come. Paddy was suffering from a writer's block that was to last for the rest of his life.[21] In her biography of Paddy, his friend Artemis Cooper writes that he believed 'the whole subject was beginning to feel stale, barren, written out, and he feared he no

---

* 'Patrick Leigh Fermor' was the fourteenth episode of season twelve of the TV arts magazine, *The South Bank Show* broadcast on London Weekend Television on 22 January 1989.

† Major Alexander Fielding, writer, traveller and wartime spy, worked for the Special Operations Executive with Paddy in German-occupied Crete in 1941, and met Joan, with Paddy, in Cairo three years later. He died in Paris in January 1991, leaving a widow, 'Mougouch' (an Armenian term of endearment for 'little mighty one', and usually misspelled by her friends as 'Magouche'). Born Agnes Magruder, the daughter of an old Washington family, Mougouch was previously married to the painters Arshile Gorky and Jack Phillips. She died in London on 2 June 2013.

‡ When eventually Paddy did go to stay at Sandringham, in April 1992, he went alone. Joan felt she would be superfluous, as Paddy's friend, Deborah Devonshire, was going too; besides she did not possess the requisite three evening dresses, and the house party of twenty sounded 'rather terrifying ... like a three day cocktail party.' (Fenwick, *Joan*, p. 286).

Coote and Paddy at lunch on the terrace, with the housekeeper, Rizza; Kardamyli, 1990 (Photo: Freda Berkeley).

longer had the strength to bring it back to life'. It seemed unlikely that the conclusion would ever now appear. Maybe he was paralysed by the high expectations which the success of the first two volumes had raised. For the three friends it was clear that he was, in Joan's own words, 'sadly stuck', so they avoided the subject.

The next day set the pattern for the fifteen days of their stay: a late breakfast (with Joan's home-made bitter marmalade) followed by a long lazy morning, ouzo at midday, a swim at 1 p.m. (for those who could manage the 24 steps down to the beach), and lunch at 2 p.m., on the terrace under the fig tree. After lunch Coote would smoke her cigar and read *The Times* of the previous day, while the others had a siesta – then came a walk in the surrounding olive groves, which Freda never forgot:

> *Paddy drove us up & charged ahead for his walk, while Joan & Billa & I followed in our own time, abandoning Coote for a sit on a rock. Lovely smells of mountain sage and wild thyme. It was idyllic, with the little cyclamen at our feet and the hundreds of olive trees making marvellous shapes. Then back to tea – reading*

Paddy sealing retsina bottles, Kardamyli, 1990 (Photo: Freda Berkeley).

Paddy and Coote at dinner, Kardamyli, 1990 (Photo: Freda Berkeley).

– & drinks & dinner. Meals here are simple & delicious, mostly vegetable dishes, or, if there is fish caught, then fish. Lots of v. good red wine, and ouzo; and at lunchtime retsina.

In these long and lazy days Freda was able to catch up on her reading for the first time since Lennox died. First she read Paddy's own *Mani: Travels in the Southern Peloponnese,* then L. P. Hartley's novel *The Hireling.*

It brings back so many memories, staying with Leslie [Hartley] *at Bathavon in his house by the river, & old Christabel Aberconway getting plastered, falling downstairs, & breaking her wrist.** *Billa remembers coming with Roy for a meal that weekend, and me looking after Christabel . . . The chauffeur in the book* [the 'hireling' Ledbetter, a former sergeant-major] *is so, so like Leslie's manservant & is, I'm sure, based on that one, though he always had* [as servants] *shady characters of the bullying type.*

Freda had also brought with her the diaries of Frances Partridge, but she was so affected by the author's misery on the death of her beloved husband, Ralph (ex-husband of Dora Carrington and reluctant object of Strachey's yearning love) that she had to put it down. 'Not really the thing for me at the moment', she wrote in her own diary. If only she had turned the pages back a couple of years to 1958 she would have found an entry that might have offered hope from a source within feet of where she was reading: 'This evening over our fireside dinner', Frances Partridge's diary records, 'the conversation turned to present-day pessimism, or *cafard.*† Where can one look to find enthusiasm for living? I could only think of Paddy Leigh Fermor.'[22]

The following day, after walking into the village with Billa (who

* Christabel, Lady Aberconway, widow of the 2nd Baron, died in 1974.

† Depression. *Avoir le cafard* means to feel low or down in the dumps.

then felt unwell and went to bed for the rest of the day), Freda fell into a depression, thinking about old times and about Lennox in particular – and all the things she wished she had said to him.

> *I had the first real good cry for ages. Then Joan came to see if I wanted to go for a walk & I collapsed on her shoulder. It was the nicest thing that could have happened, & an enormous relief to me – She, too, has shed endless tears as her brother . . . has the same awful thing* [as Lennox, i.e. Alzheimer's].

Freda was better by drinks at 8 p.m. and an hour later they dined – just the four of them, as Billa was still in her room:

> *Paddy was in a very relaxed & happy mood having had the Greek TV people here in the morning – They are making a programme for Ochi Day on the 28th Oct, the anniversary of the day that Greece joined the war* [in 1940, after the Greek dictator Ioannis Metaxas said '*Ochi*' (No) to an ultimatum made by Mussolini]. *The German Ambassador had left a bottle of Poireau with Rizza, which we opened.* I told Paddy about M. H.* [Father Michael Hollings, M.C., her parish priest and special friend]† *& A Time to Keep Silence & he was thrilled beyond belief.‡ At the time the book came out all the reviews were good except one by Dom Gregory Murray, who I'd met in the past & who took exception to a non-Catholic penetrating the privacy of the*

* *Poireau* – a pear spirit made by Charles Martell and Son in Gloucestershire. Rizza was the house-keeper who had recently succeeded Lela Giannakeas, and was soon to be replaced by Elpida Beloyannis. Lela, who features in so many accounts of other visits to Kardamyli, had gone on to open the waterfront taverna in Kardamyli which bears her name.

† Father Hollings was the parish priest of St Mary of the Angels, Bayswater, from 1978 till his death in 1997. A liturgical maverick, he practised the open-house philosophy he preached, and was regarded by many of his parishioners as a near saint.

‡ *A Time To Keep Silence*: travel book by Patrick Leigh Fermor, about his sojourn in four monasteries (John Murray, 1957).

*monastic life.** *So P. was enchanted to hear that Michael used it in retreats, but, even more than that, he remembered parts of it by heart.*

One evening Paddy took his friends up to a little rock-chapel above the house, and Freda noted in her diary:

> *A glorious sunset & 2 white mules being led through the olives. In the tiny building a little picture of St. Michael – rather battered – & I thought, with gratitude, of my Michaels* [Berkeley and Hollings].† *Later a delicious dinner cooked by Joan, with chicken stuffed with olives* [and roasted in the Leigh-Fermors' own green olive oil] ... *Always with Paddy lots of laughter. Much talk of the spies we knew. None of us knows Cairncross though.*‡ *I shall always remember Guy* [Burgess] *with gratitude – he was so sweet to me on Saturday nights at the Reform Club when I was painfully shy, & Anthony Blunt I liked too.*§ *Finished The Hireling – & now reading Jim Lees-Milne's book on Lord Esher – the most extraordinary story!* [about Esher's long affair with his own son, Maurice].[23]

* Benedictine monk at Downside, organist and composer; 1905–92.

† Michael was also the Greek name of Patrick Leigh Fermor – he had used 'Michalis' as his nom de guerre during the Cretan resistance, and locally he was still known as 'Kyr Mihali'. On the feast day of St Michael, 8 November, according to Paddy's own account, 'the whole village comes up here [the rock chapel above the Leigh Fermor house] to attend mass ... Then they troop along to the house for liqueurs and sweet cakes' – Adam Sisman (ed.), *Dashing for the Post – The Letters of Patrick Leigh Fermor*, John Murray, 2016.

‡ John Cairncross (1913–95), British civil servant and wartime spy, alleged to be the fifth member of the Cambridge Five.

§ Freda's husband Lennox had followed his father, Captain Hastings Berkeley, into membership of the Reform Club and used it throughout the war and for a decade after. He was part of a clique of well-connected homosexual men – among them Burgess and Blunt – who commandeered the upstairs Committee Room as a Saturday night meeting-place, in those days before Wolfenden when gay men lived in fear and guilt. After their marriage in 1946 Freda took care to cultivate these friends, and, by popular demand, she was invited to join them for the Reform Saturdays: the only woman in an otherwise exclusively male club. See Scotland, *Lennox & Freda*, pp 419–21.

Freda told Billa the story, and Billa claimed the book she was reading capped Freda's. It was a French biography, in French, of Medora Leigh, the alleged daughter of Byron and his half-sister Augusta Leigh.[24] Medora's life was nothing but misery, and Billa spared Freda no details. In her teens Medora had been seduced by her sister's husband, bore his child, was placed in an asylum, and escaped with her seducer to Brittany, where she had another child, a daughter who later became a nun. Abandoned a second time, she worked on a farm for a while, then took a job as housekeeper to a French army officer. When he too cast her aside, she settled down with his batman in the hills of Aveyron in southern France, where she bore a son, Byron's grandson, who became a Catholic priest. Medora died of smallpox in 1849 and is buried in Versols-et-Lapeyre. Billa said she could not imagine Byron's grandchildren being Catholics; Freda said she could not imagine the Church receiving them.*

Great excitement on Thursday the 18th, feast day of Saint Luke the Evangelist, patron saint of artists, physicians, bachelors, surgeons, students and butchers, when the Metropolitan of Gytheion and Oitylo descended on Kardamyli with hosts of priests and acolytes and altar boys for a celebratory Mass in the Church of St. Spyridon. Paddy drove the ladies to the village church to join in:

> *The Metropolitan very fine, with flowing robes, long beard, & a wonderful tiara. It was very, very moving, with the relics exposed, the chanting & the Blessings. Paddy got candles for us all which we lit outside the church & stuck in sand. When we emerged we were all given chunks of holy bread from huge round loaves. Billa & I followed the procession ... and the Metropolitan turned & blessed the 2 of us again. Someone took a bag of the bread around*

---

* One of Byron's other illegitimate children, Allegra (his daughter by Claire Clairmont) died in a Catholic convent where, as a sick child, she had been placed by Byron himself.

Right: Billa, Kardamyli, 1990 (Photo: Freda Berkeley).

Below: The grave of Medora Leigh at Versols-et-Lapeyre, which the ladies visited on their return journey. A tablet erected in the 1960s bears a line from Byron's *Childe Harold's Pilgrimage*: 'Strangers not regardless pass, lingering like me to gaze and sigh "Alas!"' (Photo: Freda Berkeley).

Below right: Church of St. Spyridon, Kardamyli (Photo: Freda Berkeley).

the village for the shopkeepers. Bells were ringing, rung by 2 small boys with tremendous zest.

No one who has read Paddy's books – one of them about the monastic life, and two culminating in great religious events – would be surprised by his fascination with religious ceremonial and even, for all his reluctance ever to examine his own feelings, with spiritual feelings. If Freda seems to have responded to the Orthodox Masses with the same enthusiasm it was because she had recently returned to the Roman Catholic Church with renewed faith, having originally converted – largely from a sense of duty to Lennox – while she was carrying their first son, Michael. Being away from home, surrounded by old friends, freed her to think of the past, and this unleashed a stream of mixed memories:

The enormous leap for me this past year has been back to the Church again. L. wd be so happy & I know he's behind it. When the boys were young all was well, but then, with that awful, awful period of restless unhappiness which I now so deeply regret, I grew away. And L. so wonderful & understanding. I really grew up with him, & through him, whereas he, being 43 when we married, had quite a past behind him. I can't think why he ever married me. Someone like June [Catholic wife of the Liberal lawyer Jeremy Hutchinson]* *would have been so much more suitable for him. But it worked, & we loved each other deeply & lastingly till his death. And now it is just me & I must do what he would want me to do ... He always said he worried about the future*

* Jeremy Hutchinson, Q.C. was one of the greatest advocates of his time, and the model for John Mortimer's television character *Rumpole of the Bailey*. His clients included the publishers of *Lady Chatterley's Lover*, Christine Keeler and the Soviet spy George Blake. His first wife was the actress Dame Peggy Ashcroft, and in 1966 he married June Osborn, posthumous daughter of Captain Arthur 'Boy' Capel, and granddaughter of Lord Ribblesdale. In 1978 Jeremy was created a life peer as Baron Hutchinson of Lullington. June died in 2006, and Jeremy followed her in 2017, aged 102.

for me – that he would want me to marry again ... to make a lovely new life for myself. Perhaps, but first I must put the old one behind me ...

However much the spirit of Lennox might have wished for Freda's return to the Church, it was Father Michael Hollings who all but frogmarched her back to Mass, when, after Lennox's death, she came to live in Hereford Mansions, within sight of his church. Not for nothing was he known as 'Stonker' during his wartime service with the Coldstream Guards; as Major Hollings, aged only twenty, he won the MC for extraordinary devotion to duty after being shot through the throat during a night attack in Tunis in 1942. Freda first met him at Westminster Cathedral, when her sons were at the choir school, and was then a little frightened of him. But helping people was his mission, and when she needed help during Lennox's last illness, it was he who came to the rescue, supporting her through those difficult times, saying a weekly Mass at Lennox's bedside and celebrating the Latin Requiem Mass at his funeral in the Church of Our Lady, Lisson Grove. On Freda's move to Bayswater, a few months later, Father Hollings became not only her parish priest but a firm friend.

The relationship was to deepen in 1996 when he was suspended from his parish, following a newspaper story that he had molested a young man years previously. The police were informed, he was locked out of his presbytery and, with nowhere else to go, he moved in with Freda for six months. When at last the police dropped the case for lack of evidence, and the Westminster diocese re-instated Father Hollings at St. Mary of the Angels, the congregation spontaneously applauded the return of their beloved priest, and Cardinal Hume came to say Mass. But it was all too late. Diabetes had taken a hold, and Father Hollings died a few months later on 21 February 1997.

The 'period of restless unhappiness', which Freda touches on in

Freda at home at Hereford Mansions, and Fr Michael Hollings at Hereford Mansions (Photos: Tony Scotland).

her travel diary, probably refers to the middle years of her marriage, when Lennox was holed up in his study, composing, for most of every day, and the three boys were away at school. Freda, still barely forty, was at a loose end and looking for something to do. Meeting the bachelor eye-surgeon Patrick Trevor-Roper, she accepted his invitation to play hostess at his official parties in London for the International Academy of Ophthalmology and the Royal Society of Medicine, and his weekend parties for his medical students at the country house he shared in Wiltshire. Pat was clever, witty, anarchic, unusually well-connected and a pioneer of gay activism. Freda fell under his spell and soon developed a deep affection which lasted for some years. Lennox knew and accepted this, though he was puzzled – and once or twice unintentionally hurt: hence Freda's regrets. But all came right, since nothing much had gone wrong. And Freda never did re-marry.

These were the thoughts that filled her mind in the first week of the Kardamyli holiday, but such was the balm of the company of old friends that, having conjured up these challenging memories and committed them to paper, she felt she had shed a great burden.

Five nights into the fortnight, just as life with the Leigh Fermors was settling into a delightfully predictable routine, the Athens bus delivered a lively newcomer, clever, sympathetic and playful:

A charming young writer who is doing a biography of Robert Byron arrived from Athens at about 9 p.m. He is called James Knox & his wife works at Murray's. * *Had a v. late delicious dinner at about 10.30 & lots of drink before.*

The new arrival strengthened the gender balance in Paddy's favour, and he took advantage by marching James up into the hills the next afternoon. According to Freda they were all much taken by the young visitor – just as James Lees-Milne had been when James Knox consulted him about Byron earlier the same year. Lees-Milne's diary records him as 'That charmer Knox . . . Very good-looking; slight; little cow-lick on side of hair. White teeth, white skin, white cuffs, thin white hands . . . Very keen on Robert . . . Is clearly intelligent, with a quick grasp . . . '.[25]

Paddy had known Robert Byron before the war when they were both Bright Young People, and he had long admired his travel books – particularly *The Station*, recording an epic journey to the monasteries of Mount Athos – and took inspiration from his gift for hilarious narrative. But Joan and Billa and Coote had known Byron better. Joan, who was then studying Persian art, travelled to Russia with him in 1935 to attend an international congress on Persian art and archaeology at the Hermitage Museum in Leningrad; Billa saw a lot of him in 1937 when she was Secretary of the Georgian Group which Byron had helped to found; and Coote knew Byron as one of the principals of the parties at Madresfield, to which he

---

* Caroline Knox was then Senior Editor in John Murray's biography, history and travel team. Later she founded the Boswell Book Festival, held each May at Auchinleck House, Ayrshire, home of the first great modern biographer, James Boswell.

Robert Byron (passport, 1923).

had been introduced through his Eton friendship with her brother Hugh. Only Freda had never known Byron, for he had died in 1941 when his ship was torpedoed in the North Atlantic and she was at secretarial school, but she remembered Lennox talking about him for they had matriculated at Oxford in the same term, and in the same college, Merton. (Joan's brother, Graham, was also a Merton man.) Knox was delighted to have a chance to interview four of his subject's contemporaries simultaneously, so that each could jog the others' memories, and they were no less delighted by his enthusiastic and well-informed interest. When the biography of Byron came out in 2003 Paddy recommended it in *The Spectator*'s Christmas list as 'a book we have been waiting years for, and it surpasses all expectations'.[26]

According to James Knox that Kardamyli weekend involved the consumption of a lot of wine with much jolly talk, peppered with extravagant compliments about Joan's cooking and Paddy's stories, all of it accompanied by 'appreciative "darling"s, superlatives, gasps of surprise and unfinished sentences'. If the conversation fell short of dazzling, it was because these were old, old friends, familiar with one another's foibles, fables and feelings: there was nothing much to say that had not been said before – it was enough just to bask in the warmth of shared experiences, gossiping about other old friends.

James remembers that Paddy swam for half an hour every morning, making for the rocky island in the bay below the house, and he could not help noticing that Joan was quiet, withdrawn and in low spirits. In this she was not alone. Paddy was given to fits of depression too. So was Freda, and at least twice during the fortnight at Kardamyli she woke with what she calls 'one of my panics'. She had left behind her supply of Valium tablets, so she had to resort to the Edward Bach herbal, 'Rescue Remedy' (made of rock rose, impatiens, clematis, Star of Bethlehem and cherry plum). Freda trusted it to dispel the blues, but it never did – nor could it. On the 22nd she wrote:

> *This was one of those mornings when my awful inferiority complex takes over completely & I become painfully shy & inarticulate . . . L. always knew & understood & wd soothe me. He was always so loving & so wise & so clever, & never minded that I wasn't clever too.*

Another panic on waking on the 27th, but this time one of Joan's cats came to the rescue.

> *Woke feeling desolate with an unaccountable fear of something awful happening. It was quite comforting when I opened my shutters v. early & there was Johnny asking to come in, with tremendous purring & making up to me, & then diving into the bottom of my bed.*

Cats were a passion of Joan's, though not of Paddy's. A friend staying once counted 73. They lived in Joan's bedroom, even in her bed, and were not averse to other people's beds too. Joan used to warn her friends in advance, but that did not prevent occasional accidents. At supper one night she said that when Freda's son, Michael, was staying in 1975, one of the cats made a mess on his bed, which he then sat on. Freda said that actually the cats had also sprayed his rucksack and everything in it, but he only discovered it on the bus afterwards – en route to Athens to stay with the British

Ambassador, Sir Brooks Richards. Joan begged Freda to invite Michael to come and stay again to make up for it.

Music, literature and chess were other addictions of Joan's. A young friend who once slept in her room while she was away – entry was strictly forbidden when she was there – recalled his astonishment at the range and depth of the literature on her shelves. They included cookery books, a large section on chess, poetry and works on Eastern philosophy – all somewhat tainted by the smell of cats. When she was not reading or knitting or listening to music, Joan could be found playing chess on her pocket set. She would not play with Paddy who was too impatient, so she played solo or against the computer. With guests, once she had fed them, she would withdraw into herself when Paddy held forth, or simply retire to her room – but she made an exception for Billa, Coote and Freda.

There were outings through the rocky Deep Mani to Vathia ('rather spoiled'), to Mezapos ('the pirates' port') and Gerolimenas, Harouda, the fishing village of Agios Nikolaos, and lunches at Lela's Taverna. All the while Paddy explaining things, telling stories, chatting to the locals in Greek, singing songs and even dancing.

On the last full day of their trip, Sunday the 28th, Paddy raised the blue-white Greek flag beside the Union Flag to mark *Ochi* Day and the Greek defiance of Hitler in 1940.

> *We all went down to the village where there was a service in the church, everyone in their best, & P. & J. lined up with the Mayor. They had to go & have coffee after, & Billa & I walked up to the old village – v. peaceful & serene. P. & B. swam afterwards, then we drove up to Pyrgi, lovely village in the hills, & had delicious mezze & fish, sitting out on the terrace with a glorious view.*

That evening, before the three ladies retired to bed, Joan put on some music. Perhaps because they were all still in a wistful mood after the *Ochi* memorial service, she chose to play a recording of the

Joan Leigh Fermor at Gerolimenas, 1990 (Photo: Freda Berkeley).

Memorial Requiem Mass for Lennox at Westminster Cathedral the previous March. The Mass had been celebrated by Cardinal Hume, and was broadcast live on Radio Three, with a commentary by Father Cormac Rigby. The music included Bach's chorale prelude *Herzlich tut mich verlangen,* played on the organ by Iain Simcock, and Berkeley's own *Mass for Five Voices* sung by the Cathedral Choir.* After they had listened to it in thoughtful silence, Joan said she would like to hear it all again, and Freda left the tape with her.

* The music also comprised the second of Berkeley's *Three Pieces* for organ, his *Festival Anthem,* 'O that I once past changing were' and the motet *Ubi caritas,* with Michael Berkeley's *Qui me dignatus est.* The address was given by Bishop Gordon Wheeler, Sir John Manduell paid a tribute and Tony Scotland read from the diaries of Julien Green.

Return Journey Home - Monday, 29th Oct -
We left Kardamyli about 10.15 - seen
off by Joan & Paddy - v. lovingly - &
with a 'come again' invitation for '91.
I love Joan, & understand her agony,
& feel so much more at ease with her
now. I feel, in time, we may get
very close, but there have been moments
when I've felt desperately unhappy,
likewise B & C - For Joan, I feel it's like
an extended menopause, but apparently
it's always been like this - a <u>brilliant</u>
mind, & yet agonising over everything.
When I get home I'll write her a
long letter - really long - because
I've learnt to love her -
C. wanted to take us to see Ithome
en route for Patras today. We picked
up tickets at Kalamata for the boat
& then set off - refreshed by an Ouzo.
At Messini we stopped & bought picnic
food & drink - & then set off up a very
pretty road through the mountains &

Freda's travel diary entry for the last day of their stay,' 29 October 1990.

We leave tomorrow, & the really fine weather has left too. I feel renewed in every way after my first visit to Kardamyli. Have eaten & drunk too much, read a lot &, when my foot was better, walked a lot – & perhaps thought too much. I think Paddy has one of the liveliest minds I've ever known. He is so sweet & so patient & it makes me unhappy when Joan snaps at him, which she does so often. C. & B. say she has always been like that, but has got much, much worse . . . I love Joan, & understand her agony, & feel so much more at ease with her now. I feel, in time, we may get very close, but there have been moments when I've felt desperately unhappy, likewise B. & C., for Joan. I feel it's like an extended menopause . . . a brilliant mind, & yet agonising over everything. When I get home I'll write her a long letter – really long because I've learnt to love her.

Later Freda said she thought Joan may have had reason to be snappy. Paddy was nothing if not handsome, charming, brilliant and exciting, every inch the hero, and, as John Julius Norwich put it, 'the most extraordinary literary – and social – phenomenon I have

Paddy, Kardamyli, 1990 (Photo: Freda Berkeley).

ever known',[27] but there were flaws. He could be selfish, he was often absent from home, he was a self-confessed cadger and, as his biography reveals, a serial philanderer. For decades Joan had borne all this with unconditional love and financial support, but she would not have been human if sometimes her patience wore thin.

Artemis Cooper suggests that Joan was the Wendy to Paddy's Peter Pan – the girl who flies away to Neverland to live with Peter and his band of Lost Boys in perpetual childhood. In the story Peter stays on in Neverland refusing to grow up, but Wendy leaves the island to return to the real world. Perhaps, Freda suggested, in uniting herself so closely to Paddy's life and work, by making it possible for him to write, by feeding all his needs and satisfying all his whims, Joan had sacrificed her own intellectual and artistic gifts.

She may have sacrificed motherhood too. Certainly she never did have children, though it is clear she wanted them. With John Rayner she had a miscarriage; with Paddy she had hopes of multiple motherhood. In a letter of 1948, when she was in London and Paddy was staying at the Abbaye de Solesmes, gathering material for *A Time To Keep Silence*, she made no bones about it. She was longing for his return, she wrote, so they could set off on a motoring holiday to Sicily, before settling down 'in our own Georgian country house', where 'I shall have tiny Fermors every year (if we ever get married)'.[28] But when they did marry they slept in separate bedrooms for the remaining 35 years of Joan's life. Paddy wanted freedom and the solitude to write and create, and Joan made it possible. In spite of everything she adored him, knew he needed her – as she needed him and his understanding, for, by her own admission, she was a grumbler, somewhat aloof, not always sweet-tempered, and chronically indecisive. On the last page of her pocket diary for 1936 her biographer, Simon Fenwick, reveals that she scribbled some lines of doggerel in which she criticises herself for never being able to make up her mind: 'Crowds? Alone? "I don't know" cries Schizo Joan'.

XII

Home

On the morning of Monday the 29th October the visitors packed up for home. Undaunted by the two thousand miles that lay ahead, Coote supervised the loading of the car. Billa had collected two Greek caterpillars for her grandson, Hugo, and took care to pack them in a cardboard box lined with damp sand, a couple of sticks to climb on, some fresh leaves to nibble, and ventilation holes pricked in the sides.* She was equally careful with a jar of local honey which Joan gave her as a present for the Prince of Wales, placing both the bug box and the royal honey in the glove pocket in front of her. Freda arranged herself in the back, walking sticks and handbags were stowed away, and the three set off for England, in a flurry of waves and cries of 'Come again next year'.

It took them longer than expected to reach Patras because they got lost looking for the village of Ithomi and the archaeological remains of Theban Messene, which Joan had urged them not to miss. So it was peak rush-hour and dark when they arrived at the port, and in the chaos of the traffic they could not find the ferry terminal. Freda set off on foot to look for the boat, and at last, in an unlit and sinister street, she found the offices of the ferry company, and was directed to the quay.

Coote just managed to reach the ferry in time for the ten o'clock

---

* Both caterpillars arrived in England safely, and pupated in Billa's lush garden at The Old Rectory in Holt. On 4 December 1990 she wrote to Joan to report that her grandson was thrilled with the two chrysalises and was planning 'a glamorous cage for their short life' when they emerged as moths in the Spring. (Sir Patrick Leigh Fermor Archive, National Library of Scotland.)

crossing to Italy. They were sailing this time in the *Poseidonia* – roomier cabins than on the *Ouranos*, but there was a bit of movement on the sea and Billa was very sick. For Freda there was a consolation prize after her chase through the dark streets of Patras: 'a charming young steward', who took her under his wing as she stepped aboard, carried her bags to the cabin, then accompanied her to the restaurant where she and Coote and Billa had 'a rather bad meal', while the young man continued to dance attendance. After frequent re-appearances to check she was all right, he carried her bags down the gangway when they docked at Brindisi – then asked if he could kiss her. 'Came onto the quay,' Freda records with delight, '& kissed me again – twice!! Felt ten years younger, others greatly amused.'

Freda cast a spell on everyone she met – men, women, young, old. Earlier in 1990, at the end of a gay luncheon party with friends in Notting Hill Gate, she threw her feet into the lap of a Belgian baron, for a massage, and, to her astonishment, he rang the next day to declare his love. This was 'the sort of thing that always happens to me', she recalled in the Greek diary, '& cheers me up to think of it – it's so funny!'

Reluctantly deciding they would have to spend the night in Brindisi, Billa booked them into a central hotel, about which not even Coote could find anything positive to say. It was, she wrote to Joan when she got home:[29]

> *... all marble & looking glass & really nasty food, for all of which they charged les yeux de la tête, & full of Mafia, really sinister Rififi figures sitting watching telly in the dark.**

* Coote was referring to the 1955 French crime film, *Du rififi chez les hommes*, about a gang of thugs who rob a jeweller's shop in the rue de Rivoli; 'rififi' was underworld slang for a pitched battle.

They were thankful to escape the next morning and head for Ortona, stopping in Termoli for a fish lunch which Coote, an accomplished cook herself, described with relish:

> *We had crostini with fish first, then each a small oval dish with a sole, a whiting, a skewer of Kalamares, Dublin bay prawns split down the middle, & one other thing (? mussels), all grilled & hopping fresh.*

After Ortona and l'Aquila they spent two nights in Assisi, where it was difficult to find a hotel because they coincided with the feasts of All Saints and All Souls when the whole of Italy returns to the country to take flowers to its dead, so 'we had to sleep 3 in an attic – to Billa's indignation'. But Freda slipped out to buy a bottle of whisky to soften the blow.

In Borgo San Sepolcro they saw the *Resurrection* by Piero della Francesca (described by Aldous Huxley as the greatest painting in the world); in Monterchi, at Billa's insistence they found the same artist's pregnant Madonna; at the Bacci Chapel in the hill town of Arezzo, Piero's fresco cycle the *Legend of the True Cross*, and 'a tremendous thieves' kitchen bazaar in progress with flame eaters & jugglers, all very mediaeval'; and in Rubiera, Coote wrote:

We fought our way into the Clinica Gastronomica at the Golden Eagle ... The menu exactly the same as when I was there about 25 yrs ago. Very good hors d'oeuvres, various pastas & bollito misto or carne al forno with pesto etc. We got into conversation with a nice Polish professor [who] *had just been to Russia, of wh. he takes a very gloomy view & said it was deeply depressing.*[30]

Leaving their car at the hotel in Rubiera (and accidentally leaving the keys in the driver's door; kindly rescued by the concierge), they took the bus to Modena, to see the celebrated Duomo. Coote was unimpressed: 'Cathedral OK', she wrote to Joan. But it left its mark on Freda:

Cathedral shut till 3.30. However we eventually got in. V. early Romanesque – great atmosphere & tranquillity. I only hope all the prayers for Lennox go up with the candles I've lit for him, also the family and M. [Hollings].

On Tuesday the 6th November, they drove on to the Piedmont village of Bussoleno, where 'Freda sussed out a good upstairs restaurant for lunch', Coote recalled, adding in admiration, 'she has a nose like a pointer!' From there they made their way to the Fréjus road tunnel and on into France, up and down the *col* of the *Dent du Chat*, as Coote wrote in her thank-you letter to Joan:

The Mont Cenis road was really lovely with a lot of fresh snow on top. We flopped into a village called St. Maurice de Maurienne just before dark, bitterly cold -5° centigrade. Hotel so-so. The next day we drove out of the mountains & through all the Beaujolais Villages, pausing at Juliénas to buy a case of wine between us. Here, as elsewhere, everybody poured out their life stories to Freda & Billa.[31]

Via Paray-le-Monial, a noisy night in Saint-Florentin, and a modern motel in Noyen-sur-Seine, they reached Calais on Saturday the 10th, spent the night in the Hotel Ibis and caught the first hovercraft the next morning – 'only 35 min. over the Channel so because of the time [difference] we arrived before we left & were in London by 12'.

Coote dropped Freda and Billa at Hereford Mansions and drove on down to Faringdon for lunch with a friend; Henry Harrod came to collect his mother; and Freda was on her own – but cheered up by a Welcome Home banner over the front door, and flowers in the kitchen which had been reconstructed in her absence.

All three wrote enthusiastic bread-and-butter letters to Joan. Billa's said:

> *We all adored being at Kardamyli so much; it is always absolute heaven to be there with you & Paddy, it is a divine & perfect house and you make it so tremendously enjoyable. I like it better than anywhere I know. A thousand thanks for having three fat & greedy ladies for a whole fortnight.*[32]

Freda wrote in her diary:

> *Our trip was an enormous success against all odds – 3 females, & me 12 yrs younger than the others. But Coote was the key ... She achieved it all for us.*

Billa felt the same:

> *Our drive back was wonderful, no accidents and no cross words. Coote is the most remarkable person I know: so clever, so knowledgeable, so full of energy . . . and so calm.*[33]

With her active social life and further foreign travels, her garden and her cottage, Coote had plenty to keep her busy. Billa, with her family, the Norfolk Churches and church crawls with the Prince of Wales, was, if anything, even busier. Both she and Coote were independent, purposeful and self-motivated. Freda, though no less of an optimist, shared none of her friends' enterprise, and needed constant company to see off the black dog. But she was uncomplaining about herself and full of curiosity about others, so she was much sought-after and always ready for anything her friends might suggest.

Waiting for her in a pile of post on the hall table were two letters in handwriting she recognised immediately and gladly. One was from her younger friend, the children's publisher Sebastian Walker, inviting her to Munich the following weekend; the other was from her older friend, Pat Trevor-Roper, inviting her to the country the weekend after that. So she was not forgotten. She was also in daily contact with her three sons and their families, her young friends Robert Annibale and Edesio Fernandes and their neighbours' network in Hereford Mansions; besides, there was her special relationship with Father Michael Hollings – and a new romantic friendship about to start with Alec Guinness.

For Freda, despite increasing immobility, life was still a joyride; for the busy widows Billa and Coote too. But they all worried about Paddy and Joan, and had reflected on this at length on the way home. For all his celebrity, Paddy was locked in writer's block and unable to complete his life's work; this must have depressed him to the point of despair. And beautiful, clever, romantic Joan, his muse and collaborator, the hero's heroic enabler, was just as stuck: locked in Paddy's legend, she had never found the focus to identify what might have been her own life's work. But they still had each other and their grand creation at Kardamyli, and, if the circle of old friends was necessarily contracting as the years went by, the circle of admirers and fans was growing – and would continue to grow long after Paddy went to his rest beside Joan in the churchyard at Dumbleton.

ACKNOWLEDGEMENTS

This book was inspired by conversations with the late Freda Berkeley, and her Kardamyli travel diary. She hoped that her notes and spoken memories could be worked into a story based on the threads of friendship and shared experience which linked the five friends pictured within. The author is especially grateful to Julian Berkeley, Adam Bager, John Byrne and Sidney Buckland for reading the initial drafts, correcting errors and suggesting improvements; to Susan Wightman of Libanus Press for setting and designing the book; to Sarah Godsill for the dustjacket illustration; and for additional help: Michael Berkeley, Michael Bloch, Robert Annibale and Edesio Fernandes, Joey Casey, the late Jane Norman, Selina Hastings, Colin Heber-Percy, Philippa Jellicoe, James Knox, and David McClay and Kirsty McHugh (Curators, John Murray Archive [including the Sir Patrick Leigh Fermor Archive], National Library of Scotland, Edinburgh).

SOURCES

1 Michael Berkeley, 'We lived in a secret, intoxicating world', *The Guardian*, 10 February 2003.

2 For further accounts of the work of the Allied photo reconnaissance squadrons in the Foggia airfields during WWII, see: Jane Wilson, *On Wing & Water: the Life of Leslie R. Colquhoun, War Hero ...*, Cirencester, Mereo Books, 2014; Thomas K. Follis, *He Wore a Pair of Silver Wings: The World War II Memoir of a Lightning Recon Pilot*, Bennington, Vermont, Merriam Press, 2004; and Dave Humphrey, *Legends & Heroes – Behind the Lens*, Raleigh, North N.C., Rossendale Books, 2014.

3 Charlotte Mosley (ed.), *In Tearing Haste: Letters Between Deborah Devonshire and Patrick Leigh Fermor*, John Murray, 2009.

4 Hermione, Countess of Ranfurly, *To War With Whitaker: The Wartime Diaries of the Countess of Ranfurly, 1939–45*, William Heinemann, 1994.

5 Byrne, Paula, *Mad World: Evelyn Waugh and the Secrets of Brideshead*, Harper, 2010.

6 David Wykes, *Evelyn Waugh: A Literary Life*, Springer, 2016, p. 141.

7 Jane Mulvagh, *Madresfield: The Real Brideshead*, Doubleday, 2008, p. 372.

8 *Ibid.*, p. 40.

9 Billa confessed this years later to her friend, the designer Jaime Parladé, who passed it on to Simon Fenwick in 2017. See Simon Fenwick, *Joan: The Remarkable Life of Joan Leigh Fermor*, Macmillan, 2017, p. 78.

10 Letter Patrick Leigh Fermor to Deborah Devonshire, *In Tearing Haste*, 6 December 1977.

11 Lady Harrod, obituary of Joan Leigh Fermor, *The Daily Telegraph*, 5 July 2003.

12 Cyril Connolly's description, quoted by Fenwick, *Joan*, p. 169.

13 Fenwick, *Joan*, pp. 41 and 50.

14 Letter John Betjeman to Alan Pryce-Jones, 18 February 1935, *John Betjeman: Letters*, vol 1, p. 117.

15 Letter John Betjeman to Billa Cresswell, n.d. [February 1933], *ibid.*, p. 96.

16 Obituary of Lady Harrod, *Daily Telegraph*, 12 May 2005.

17 See, *in multis aliis libris*, Tony Scotland, *Lennox & Freda*, pp. 86–7 and 89.

18 Paddy's description, in a letter to Janetta Parladé – Fenwick, *Joan*, p. 127.

19 Letter Billa Harrod to Joan Leigh Fermor, 19 August, 1990, Sir Patrick Leigh Fermor Archive, National Library of Scotland.

20 Letter Billa Harrod to Joan Leigh Fermor, 4 December, 1990, Sir Patrick Leigh Fermor Archive, National Library of Scotland.

21 After Leigh Fermor's death, his biographer Artemis Cooper and the novelist and travel writer Colin Thubron worked on a preliminary draft he had written in the 1960s together with other manuscript notes, and in 2013 the final volume of the trilogy was published by John Murray as *The Broken Road*.

22 Partridge, Frances (ed. Rebecca Wilson), *Diaries 1939–1972*, Phoenix Press, 2001, p. 267.

23 James Lees-Milne, *The Enigmatic Edwardian: a Life of Reginald, 2nd Viscount Esher*, Sidgwick & Jackson, 1986.

24 Frédéric Jacques Temple, *Le Tombeau de Medora*, Editions de Paris, 2000.

25 Lees-Milne, James (ed. Michael Bloch), *Ceaseless Turmoil: Diaries, 1988–1992*, p. 63.

26 James Knox, *Robert Byron: A Biography* was published by John Murray in 2003.

27 John Julius Norwich, 'Patrick Leigh Fermor, my hero', *The Oldie*, April 2018.

28 Fenwick, *Joan*, p. 188.

29 Letter Coote Heber-Percy to Joan Leigh Fermor, 14 November 1990 (Sir Patrick Leigh Fermor Archive, National Library of Scotland

30 *Ibid*.

31 *Ibid*.

32 Letter Billa Harrod to Joan Leigh Fermor, 13 November 1990 (Sir Patrick Leigh Fermor Archive, National Library of Scotland).

33 *Ibid*.

BIBLIOGRAPHY

Amory, Mark, 'Obituary of Lady Dorothy Heber-Percy', *The Independent*, 20 November 2001.

Arapoglou, Evita (ed.), *Ghika-Craxton-Leigh Fermor – Charmed Lives in Greece*, Nicosia, A. G. Leventis Gallery, 2nd revised edition, 2017.

Benaki Museum Press Release, 'A new, significant grant from the Stavros Niarchos Foundation to the Benaki Museum, for the Patrick and Joan Leigh Fermor House in Kardamyli', Benaki Museum, Athens.

Berkeley, Lady [Freda], unpublished manuscript notebook recording a car journey with Lady Dorothy Heber-Percy and Lady [Billa] Harrod from London to Kardamyli and back, 3 October to 11 November 1990, Estate of the late Lady Berkeley.

Berkeley, Michael, 'We lived in a secret, intoxicating world', *The Guardian*, 10 February 2003.

Betjeman, John (ed. Candida Lycett Green), *John Betjeman: Letters*, Volume 1: 1926–1951, Volume 2: 1951–1984, Methuen, 2006.

Byrne, Paula, *Mad World: Evelyn Waugh and the Secrets of Brideshead*, Harper, 2010.

Cooper, Artemis, *Patrick Leigh Fermor – An Adventure*, John Murray, 2012.

Downing, Ben, 'A Visit With Patrick Leigh Fermor', *The Paris Review*, 17 and 24 May 2013.

Duggan, Michael, 'Roads less travelled: Patrick Leigh Fermor lived an adventurer's life', *Irish Examiner*, 7 June 2016, posted as 'Paddy's Irishness' on the Patrick Leigh Fermor blog at https://patrickleighfermor.org

Eade, Philip, *Evelyn Waugh: A Life Revisited*, Hachette UK, 2016.

Fenwick, Simon, *Joan: The Remarkable Life of Joan Leigh Fermor*, Macmillan, 2017.

Halsall, Christine, *Women of Intelligence: Winning the Second World War with Air Photos*, The History Press, 2012.

Hastings, Lady Selina, *Evelyn Waugh: A Biography*, Sinclair-Stevenson, 1994.

___, 'House of Memories' [recalling her 1989 meeting with Mona, Countess Beauchamp, mistress of Madresfield], *The Spectator*, 2 September 2009.

Kittmer, John [former UK Ambassador to the Hellenic Republic], 'From Mystras to Kardamyli – a hike in honour of Sir Patrick Leigh Fermor', published in the Foreign Office blog, *Greek Blogyssey*, 3 June 2015, at https://blogs.fco.gov.uk/greekblogyssey/

Knox, James, *Robert Byron: A Biography*, John Murray, 2003.

Lees-Milne, James (ed. Michael Bloch), *Ceaseless Turmoil: Diaries, 1988–1992*, John Murray, 2008.

Leigh Fermor, Patrick, *Mani: Travels in the Southern Peloponnese*, John Murray, 1958.

Lister, Elizabeth, 'WAAF Arm Chair Spies', *WW2 People's War: an archive of World War Two memories, written by the public, gathered by the BBC*, available online at http://www.bbc.co.uk/history/ww2peopleswar/stories/70/a7517270.shtml

Mendelsohn, Daniel, 'The Inspired Voyage of Patrick Leigh Fermor' [a review of *The Broken Road*], *The New York Times Book Review*, 19 June 2014.

Mitford, Nancy, *Love in a Cold Climate*, Hamish Hamilton, 1949.

___, *The Pursuit of Love*, Hamish Hamilton, 1945.

Mosley, Charlotte (ed.), *In Tearing Haste: Letters Between Deborah Devonshire and Patrick Leigh Fermor*, John Murray, 2009.

Mount, Harry, 'Playing Away', a review of Sisman (ed.), *Dashing for the Post*, in the *Literary Review*, October 2016.

Mulvagh Jane, *Madresfield: The Real Brideshead*, Doubleday, 2008.

Norwich, John Julius, 'Paddy the Great, king of Greece', Episode 11 of *The Oldie* Podcast – John Julius Norwich in conversation with Harry Mount.

___, *Paddy's World*, transcript of a talk given to members of the Patrick Leigh Fermor Society at the Hellenic Centre, London, 10 November 2015, posted on the Patrick Leigh Fermor blog at https://patrickleighfermor.org

___, 'Patrick Leigh Fermor, my hero', *The Oldie*, April 2018.

Page, Norman, *An Evelyn Waugh Chronology*, Palgrave Macmillan, 1997.

Pryce-Jones, Alan (ed. John Byrne, with an Introduction by David Pryce-Jones), *Devoid of Shyness: From the Journal 1926–1939*, York, Stone Trough Books, 2016.

Pryce-Jones, David, *Fault Lines*, New York, Criterion Books, 2015.

Sawford, Tom, 'The Benaki comes out fighting – progress at Paddy's house', and other articles about the Leigh Fermors and their house at Kalamitsi, posted on the Patrick Leigh Fermor blog at https://patrickleighfermor.org

Scotland, Tony, *Lennox & Freda* [the early lives, courtship and marriage of Sir Lennox Berkeley and Freda Bernstein], Michael Russell, 2010

___, (With a Foreword by Patrick Leigh Fermor), *The Empty Throne: The Quest for an Imperial Heir in the People's Republic of China* (Viking, 1993).

Sisman, Adam (ed.), *Dashing for the Post – The Letters of Patrick Leigh Fermor* (John Murray, 2016).

Vlasto, Helen, 'The "Season" of 1939', *London Portrait Magazine*, April 1984, republished at christopherlong.co.uk

Waugh, Evelyn, *Brideshead Revisited*, A Revised Edition, With A New Preface, Chapman & Hall, 1960.

___, *Vile Bodies*, Chapman & Hall, 1930.

Wheeler, Sara, 'How can one live as a sponger?', part of a review of Adam Sisman (ed.), *Dashing for the Post*, in *The Guardian*, 4 October, 2016, posted on the Patrick Leigh Fermor blog at https://patrickleighfermor.org

Zinovieff, Sofka, *The Mad Boy, Lord Berners, My Grandmother and Me*, Jonathan Cape, 2014.